Dedicated To My Mother

Clara Emilia Hahn

In appreciation
for all the hours spent in the kitchen
teaching a young child that cooking
provides not only food
but that it can give
pleasure and grace
to last a lifetime

OTHER BOOKS BY DURDEN-NELSON

Sixty years
AT HOME ...

AT THE RANGE
238 Favorite Recipes (old & new)

Plus stories about
Cooking in an old-time kitchen

A DAUGHTER'S HERITAGE
The Texas-German Approach
To The Joy of Good Basic Cooking

By
Mae Durden-Nelson

FIRST EDITION
Copyright © 2011 by Mae Durden-Nelson
Printed in the United States of America
By Nortex Press — A Division of Sunbelt Media, Inc.
P.O. Box 21235 ☜ Waco, Texas 76702
email: sales@eakinpress.com
💻 website: www.eakinpress.com 💻
ALL RIGHTS RESERVED.
1 2 3 4 5 6 7 8 9
ISBN 13: 978-1-935632-23-8
ISBN 10: 1-935632-23-X
Library of Congress Control Number 2011942413

Contents

Introduction

I marinate my wrinkled sagging skin with costly oils and cream; I take expensive Celebrex for my aching arthritic joints; and I continue to spend too much money on "covering up" my graying hair with a lovely natural shade of brown. But the calendar still confirms that I am 79 years old. Nevertheless, I continue to dream on in happy denial. I may be that old but I don't feel that aged. But then comes this elephant into the room: Not only are my children requesting, but also now my grandchildren, ". . . you know, the recipe for those cookies you used to send us while we were in college."

And this from my 56-year-old son James, "We want to make those rolled-out Christmas cookies that you and Grandma Durden always decorated."

Finally, from my forty-nine-year-old son, Roger, "Mom, do you remember when you baked my thirteenth birthday cake and it sagged in the middle? I remember how indignant you were that you had a baking failure and you had to drive twenty-five miles to the nearest grocery store to buy a cake because there was no time left before my party to bake another. We all thought it was funny that you saw no humor in that. By the way, could you send us the cookie recipe that Ruth Thomas gave you a hundred years ago?"

The final shove came when Kimberly Durden, my new *grand* daughter-in-law requested, "Josh loves that old Durden molasses cookie recipe."

"You guys! I guess my next book needs to be a heritage cookbook."

She responds, "Oh! Yes! You should do that!"

A bit of excitement rippled through me. I ought to be able to conger up enough energy for another book—number eleven!

My mind raced. I could try to recapture some of the stories as they relate to my Momma's favorite recipes. At the same time, my parallel focus could also be fun stories that relate to my own sixty years of collecting recipes. I could include some familiar sweets and dinners, family favorites, some difficult to put together but also some easy as pie. I could tell about growing up in the constant shadow of my Momma—that out of all those experiences came my love of being in the kitchen—cooking . . . and eating! It could be— a German daughter's heritage passed down. . .

Thus this book was conceived; with joy this book has been birthed.

I should give a brief one word of warning as you embark on this book. Do not, DO NOT, expect a "Julia Child" to emerge in this book. I am not a professional cook and I did not originate any of the recipes. I can guarantee, however, that I have cooked or baked every recipe included here and I can promise they are worthy of being tried in your kitchen.

—MAE DURDEN-NELSON

Preface

Where It All Began

There is nostalgia within these pages! As I allowed my memory to wander back to where all my cooking experiences began, it was amazing to realize that in Momma's farm kitchen we had only the bare essential tools for food preparation. What we did have, we did not buy. Those few shinny aluminum gadgets came to our kitchen right out of Mother's Oats, my family's favorite brand of oatmeal.

Missing from these kitchen essentials is an old long metal mixing spoon. When last seen it was half worn away from use.

As I remember it, we had only one large mixing bowl, one large mixing spoon, one flour sifter, one rolling pin, one measuring cup. Not like my modern efficient air-conditioned kitchen of today where I have two— no!—I have countless superfluous sets of kitchen gadgets that fill four large drawers and they get flim-flamed around when I'm frantic for

Only two of my four kitchen drawers filled with what every efficient kitchen *must have* today ... *if you can find it, that is!*

that one, now vital special gadget. Located just above those drawers, also in contrast with Momma's tiny kitchen, I have at ready a wonderful industrial size Kitchen Aide electric mixer equipped with three beating paddles.

This wonderful Kitchen Aide mixer was a trade-off purchase made in exchange for a first prize winner trampoline.

Which leads me to wonder: How would Mom have taken to the microwave? The convection oven? An electric bread-making machine? The blender! A food processor! CorningWare! Stainless steel, waterless cookware, and—Teflon frying pans. Momma would

Antique cast iron frying pans—seasoned inside—soot-covered outside. Eggs over easy, anyone?

have rejoiced over my fry pans. In Momma's kitchen our old cast iron Dutch oven and two well-seasoned frying pans were used morning, noon, and night. How well I remember them. Early on—as a novice dish washer—sometimes I forgot that you never washed the outside of the ironware. It was caked with years of burnton crud and soot from cooking directly over a wood fire. Yes, reflecting on the advances in kitchen technology between the 1930s and today, I am astonished.

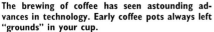
The brewing of coffee has seen astounding advances in technology. Early coffee pots always left "grounds" in your cup.

All of this inspired the writing of this blended history/recipe book. I am mindful that the patience shown by my loving mother may possibly be a bizarre story for today's mothers who perhaps eat out more than they cook. I understand that world too. Still I am grateful that my rural youthful experiences resulted in a deep love of cooking for my family and friends. If nothing else, may you take away from this succinct glimpse into that quaint yet satisfying past an appreciation for the fact that we not only survived a difficult era—but we learned many life-lessons through all of it. That training still serve us well today—in our—er—prime.

CHAPTER ONE

A Plethora of Cookies

Every year in Momma's tiny farm house kitchen, the biggest and longest cookie-baking marathon happened weeks before Christmas—all produced by the use of our wood burning range. I shake my head in disbelief to realize that we had no oven thermometer. Momma just knew! It was her acquired and learned-from-experience knowledge exactly how much wood was required in the fire chamber so as not to overheat the cast iron or allow it to become too cool to bake a perfect batch of cookies. I still hear my mother's voice, "We cannot tolerate the waste of burned cookies!"

Throughout the 1930s depression era almost all ingredients were expensive and not easy to come by. Flour was purchased in large sacks, as was white sugar. Momma began to buy and squirrel away away her cookie ingredients—little by little—throughout the year in anticipation of our cookie making marathon. Items like coconut, dates, raisins, and candied fruit for fruitcake were on this list. Pecans, another important ingredient, were harvested from the huge tree in our yard. Daddy helped with those. He sat by the fireplace in the evenings and with his sharp pocket knife he'd cut the tops, bottoms, and sides off the paper-

This old-time kitchen range gave heat for cooking—and warmth for wash-tub bath times for little children.

1

shelled pecans. Then, the entire family got involved in the final careful shelling. Momma stressed to us kids that it was important that the pecan halves be clean and whole—even though she later carefully cut up almost each kernel in neat slices. Momma also cut up her candied fruits early on and then stored all in a cool place in the pantry.

The first Christmas baking began early in the fall—like October—with fruitcakes. She stored them away to "cure" after a good soaking with some of Daddy's homemade wine.

My earliest kitchen memories begin after my older sister married and moved away. Since I was the middle child of the remaining three boy siblings—who were always outside with Daddy—I became my mother's constant shadow. While we were both big talkers, I was also taught to listen. I look back and I realize that my Momma had unbelievable patience with me—her eager, willing student—even when my lessons were not always painless. For instance, all mixing had to be done by hand with a long large metal spoon. (It eventually was half worn away with use and age!)

To demonstrate the fortitude required of all cooks in those long ago farm kitchens, come with me on a 1939 experience—step-by-step—as Momma teaches me to mix and bake my first batch of cookies.

First step is lard. "Measure it into an aluminum-measuring cup out of the large crock of lard being kept cool in our cellar."

Lard was a by-product of a once-a-year, week long winter butchering.

Those long grueling days began when a special fattened hog was slaughtered by a single shot to the head. Immediately my father stuck the hog in its juggler vein. The blood shot out in a steady stream into a large bowl that my Momma was holding with one hand while she crouched down on the dirt beside the hog. She constantly stirred the blood with the other hand to prevent clotting. That would later become an ingredient in making blood sausage.

Since the selected "butcher hog" was a very large animal, using a block and tackle, the men tugged and tugged until the hog was lifted up and then lowered into and sloshed back and forth, up and down, in a 60-gallon drum filled with boiling water.

After the hot bath was accomplished, they lifted the dead hog—then lowered it onto a low table. Immediately, several men went to work with a special sharp tool to totally shave all the bristles. Once clean shaven, again, by the use of the block and tackle, the hog was lifted into a hanging position. Now came the function of gutting and cleaning out the carcass. Some of the intestines were saved, washed and washed, then turned inside out and salted and then stored on the warm side of the wood stove until needed for later venison and pork sausage casing.

At this stage, the hog was split down the spine and the men carried the two sides inside the butchering room where it was divided into the various different cuttings of the pork. (The hog's head was usually boiled for blood sausage ingredients, or it was taken into Fredericksburg to have tamales made by local Mexicans.)

Next, daddy set aside parts for sugar-cured and smoked ham and bacon. The rest of the pork was then cut up into small pieces for grinding into sausage meat to be added to ground-up venison. The white fat layer of the hog was also cut into short strips and ground. It was later rendered—that is—it was placed in an outdoor, large black iron kettle where a hot fire underneath melted it into a liquid state—lard. When it cooled it solidified and was stored in a large crock in our cool cellar. That was our LARD supply for the entire coming year. It was a precious commodity.

Now, if I haven't lost you with all those details, let's get back to my cookies and the first ingredient: lard. To begin a batch of cookies—Momma walked with me to make that trip down into the cellar with a measuring cup and a spoon . It was a messy job! I hated it because I could not get the lard into the cup without getting it all over my hands and—well—whatever! The next step was to get the lard out of the measuring cup and into our large mixing bowl. Another messy job!

At last, the lard was placed in our large mixing bowl. The measuring cup then had to be washed with hot soapy water and carefully dried—remember—we had only one such cup.

"Measure and add the sugar," Momma instructed me, "Now mix and stir and mix and mix."

"Is this enough mixing, Momma?" I wish I had counted the "stirs."

Momma's old mixing bowl still exists. (Metal spoon is new.) If that bowl could talk ... ah ... the stories it would tell.

Momma continued, ". . . break an egg . . . one at a time . . . into a small bowl."

Momma and I give each egg the sniff test. If the smell is acceptable, "Add each egg separately . . . one at a time . . . and mix and mix and mix."

"Is this enough mixing now, Momma?"

The next step, sifting flour, was more fun. Momma always insisted that the flour had to be sifted three times before it could be correctly measured. I recall that our sifter could hold almost three cups of flour. I sifted it three times right back into the huge bag that stood against the wall in our pantry.

"Now, measure three cups of flour back into the sifter. Then, using a measuring spoon, add the salt, baking powder or baking soda, or spices . . ." (Momma purchased spices from the traveling salesman we called the "Watkins Man.")

"Now, with the sifter full of flour, salt, baking powder, or baking soda, or spices—you must sift that three times again into a separate bowl to evenly distribute everything."

"Can I mix it into the batter now, Momma?"

"No. Not yet. First we have to measure out the milk."

At last, with a tablespoon we add the flour and the milk—a little at a time—and finally we add the last ingredient: Watkins Vanilla.

Again, we mix and mix and mix. At the beginning it was quite easy to stir. After the last flour was added, Momma had to complete the process because my arms were tired! Especially with the final addition, (depending on the recipe) of the pecans or whatever else to the dough.

At last, we are ready to bake . . . that is . . . if Momma has added wood to the fire to have the temperature "just right!" She generally lets a drop of water bounce off the stove-top. She seems to know when the oven is the correct temperature. Amazing.

The aroma from baking cookies is one you will never forget! I also remember frequent swipes I sneaked out of the dough when Momma was not looking. The final reward for all this work—it was my privilege to "lick the bowl" clean after the last cookie dough was placed on the baking sheet. There was always generous dough left in the bowl. It was, you see, the age before rubber spatulas.

You probably have come to the conclusion by now that all this was hard tedious work. That's indisputable! However, at that time I guess it was just an accepted fact and it was not lamented. Day after day, Momma and I made batch after batch of cookies. All those seemingly jillions of assorted cookies were then stored away in various glass or tin containers. Momma and I regarded our accomplishment with great pride and pleasure and no one, I mean, NO ONE was allowed a sample until Christmas Eve.

Momma's Molasses Cookies*

In a large saucepan, melt $^3/_4$ cup lard over low heat and cool.

Add to melted lard:	Sift together:
1 cup white sugar	2 cups sifted flour
$^1/_4$ cup molasses	2 teaspoons baking soda
1 egg	$^1/_2$ teaspoon cloves
Beat well.	$^1/_2$ teaspoon ginger
	1 teaspoon cinnamon
	$^1/_2$ teaspoon salt
	Add to molasses mixture.

Form into 1" balls and roll in sugar. Place on greased cookie sheet 2" apart. Bake at 350 degrees 12 to 15 minutes

*From Momma's Recipe Collection

Ginger Cookies*

1 cup white sugar	1 cup molasses
1 cup brown sugar	5 cups flour
1 cup lard	3 teaspoons soda
1/2 cup water	2 teaspoons ginger

There are no instructions with this recipe.

Cornflake Cookies*

3 egg whites	2 cups Post Toasties
1 1/2 cups brown sugar	1 cup pecans
1 cup coconut	

Beat the egg whites dry. Stir in the sugar and beat hard. Then add the rest. No baking instructions.

Pineapple Cookies*

1/2 cup lard	1/4 teaspoon soda
1/2 cup brown sugar	1 teaspoon baking powder
1/2 cups drained crushed pineapple	2 cups flour
1/2 cup nuts	1 teaspoon vanilla
1 egg well beaten	1/2 cup sour milk
1/4 teaspoon salt	

Bake at 350 degrees for 15 minutes

Cocoa Cookies*

4 tablespoons lard	2 cups flour
1 cup sugar	3 teaspoon baking powder
1/4 cup milk	1/4 teaspoon salt
1 egg	1/2 cup cocoa

Cream shortening and sugar together. Add milk and beaten egg. Mix well. Sift flour, baking powder, cocoa, and salt together and add. Roll out 1/4 inch thick or drop by spoonful. Bake in hot oven about 12 minutes.

Coconut Cookies*

1/4 cup shortening	1 1/2 cups flour
1/2 cup sugar	3 teaspoon baking powder
1 egg	1/8 teaspoon salt
1/2 teaspoon lemon juice	2 cups coconut
1/2 cup milk	

Cream shortening. Add sugar, beaten egg and lemon juice. Mix in milk slowly. Add flour, baking powder and salt which have been sifted together. Add coconut. The batter should be quite stiff. Drop by small spoonfuls on greased pan. Do not smooth over, but allow space for spreading. Bake in moderate oven 15 to 20 minutes

Christmas Molasses Cookies*

1 pint dark molasses	1/2 teaspoon ginger
1 cup brown sugar	1/2 teaspoon soda dissolved in
1/2 cup lard	hot water
1/2 cup orange peel	1/2 teaspoon baking power
1/2 teaspoon cinnamon	1 egg
1/2 teaspoon allspice	

Heat molasses, add other ingredients. Add enough flour to make stiff dough. Let stand over night. Roll and cut out into shapes. Place on greased baking sheet and bake about 350 degrees.

Michigan Rocks**

1 1/2 cups sugar	1 or more cups pecans
1 cup butter, softened	1/2 teaspoon cinnamon
3 cups flour	1 1/2 teaspoon vanilla
4 eggs	1 1/2 teaspoon soda scalded
1 lb. dates	with a little hot water

Mix all ingredients well together and drop onto buttered sheet. Bake in moderate oven.

> "Broken cookies don't have calories"
> —ANONYMOUS

Half Moons*

2 cups sugar
1 cup lard
1 cup water
$^1/_2$ teaspoon soda
$^1/_2$ teaspoon salt
1 teaspoon allspice

1 teaspoon cinnamon
$^1/_2$ teaspoon cloves
1 teaspoon nutmeg
2 cups pecans
1 teaspoon baking power

Mix with enough flour to roll. Cut in half moons with biscuit cutter.

Pecan Cookie Balls*

1 cup butter
$^1/_2$ cup sifted powdered sugar
2 teaspoons vanilla
3 cups sifted flour

$^1/_4$ teaspoon salt
2 cups finely chopped pecans
Powdered sugar (about 2 cups)
 for rolling

Cream butter and add $^1/_2$ cup powdered sugar, gradually creaming. Add vanilla, flour, salt, and nuts, and blend. Chill. Shape into small balls, size of large marbles. Place on greased cookie sheet and bake in 350 degree oven about 15 minutes until just light brown. Remove from pan and at once carefully roll hot balls in sifted powdered sugar. Makes 10 dozen balls.

An Anecdote About the Author's
Sixty-Year Cookie Recipe Collection

After my family moved to Comfort in 1960, the Thomas family built a beautiful brick home down the street from us. Bill Thomas was president of Comfort's Southwestern Engineering Company, one of the largest telephone engineering firms in Texas. At the height of its success, the company employed more than one hundred people—all lived in Comfort. Southwestern was a splendid business because of the "family feeling" it promoted. Jerry Durden, my husband, was associated with this company for thirty-five years, having worked his way up from the laborious job of clearing right-of-way with an axe and a chainsaw to vice-president of outside plant.

The Thomas's had seven children, we had three, and counting the children living in our block, plus the next block—all together, there were twenty-seven kids of various ages and gender.

Being a new housing development on the outer fringe of then Comfort, during the summers the children roamed the area together in one pack and throughout the day, they wandered from one yard or house to the next. The moms were all stay-at-homes and good friends and at no time were the children left without at least one mother's eyes watching over them. The kids also knew that a batch of cookies was forthcoming in each home. No batch lasted more than a day. Ruth Thomas's cookies below were the favorite and today, fifty-one years later, they are still my now extended family's favorite.

Oatmeal Cookies *by Ruth Thomas*

2 cups shortening
  (solid Crisco, butter flavored)
2 cups light brown sugar
2 cups white sugar
4 well-beaten large eggs
2 teaspoons vanilla

3 cups flour—plus about
  $^2/_3$ cup more
2 teaspoons salt
2 teaspoons baking soda
6 cups quick cooking oatmeal
1 cup pecan meats (broken)

Cream shortening and sugars. Add well beaten eggs and vanilla. Beat.

Slowly add the dry ingredients, oatmeal and the nut meats. Store cookie dough over-night in refrigerator in a square plastic sealed container. Next day, decant onto a large cutting board and cut into 1" square cubes. Roll each cube into a ball, roll in white sugar, and place on ungreased cookie sheet. Bake at 350 degrees for 10 to 12 minutes (until light brown and surface has cracked). Makes 120 cookies.

Note: *These cookies also survived postal packaging when mailed to our "Kollege Kids." May also be frozen in a sealed freezer container.*

Another Wonderful Story
Concerning These Cookies

One day, soon after my marriage to Bill Nelson, he and I were in the middle of baking our usual double batch of Ruth's cookies. A telephone call came from some dear close friends. They inquired what we were up to and upon hearing that we were baking cookies, they said, "We'll be right over! It has been a long time since we've had home baked cookies."

They came, we visited, and I filled a medium sized box of the fresh cookies for them to take with them. Once filled, the Bishop tucked the box under his arm saying, "She will never see any of these!"

I was taken aback but decided he was only kidding. As they were getting ready to leave, I walked to her side of the car while Bill followed the Bishop to his side. I whispered to Sandy what the Bishop had said and she replied, "And he won't share them with me!"

After Bill and I returned to our kitchen, I related the story to him. We decided then it would be a fun thing to pack up a nice sized box of the cookies to mail—addressed only to 'the wife' and write that she was not to share them with the Bishop—under no circumstances!

The story goes on and on but from then on, we added the Bishop and his wife to our "Kookie Kids." Every time we mailed them we wrapped half in pink paper, half in blue.

Chocolate Crunchies

This recipe came from Suzanne Slagle who taught special education at Comfort Elementary School during the '70s. Our elementary staff often had "Fat Friday"—when everyone brought something great for that sinful event. Suzanne brought these. I've never forgotten them.

1 pkg. (6 oz) semi sweet chocolate chips
1 pkg. (6 oz) butterscotch chips

1 can (5 oz) Chinese Noodles
$^1/_2$ cup peanuts or pecans

Melt chips in double boiler. (I did this in microwave. Be careful not to overdo this process. Microwave only until they are melted.) Add noodles and pecans and mix well until everything is coated. Drop by spoonfuls onto waxed paper. Refrigerate until firm. Unusual and good.

The Newest Cookie in My Collection

Forgotten Cookies!

Planning my cookie baking for Christmas 2010, I spent a great deal of time searching the internet for something new and different. I came across this recipe—from Mrs. Claus's kitchen! It intrigued me so much that I decided to try it. Awesome discovery! It is now a permanent addition to my collection.

2 egg whites
$^3/_4$ cup sugar
1 teaspoon vanilla

1 cup semi-sweet or milk chocolate morsels
1 cup broken pecans

Preheat oven to 350 degrees. Beat egg whites to foamy soft peaks. Gradually add sugar and beat until stiff peaks can be formed. Stir in vanilla, chocolate morsels and pecans. Drop by spoonfuls onto foil-lined cookie sheets. (I didn't do this as I have Teflon cookie sheets.) Place in oven, TURN OVEN OFF, and forget cookies overnight. Pretty presentation and so good!

> "A balanced diet is a cookie in each hand."
> —ANONYMOUS

Ship Leyte Cookies

Grandma's Durden's nephew served as a cook on the US Leyte. This cookie recipe takes a lot of energy but it's worth it. Enough here to feed a ship full of sailors—or pre-schoolers!

2 ¼ cups of shortening	2 tablespoons baking powder
2 ¼ cups sugar	8 ounces shredded coconut
2 cups molasses	1 pound pecans
4 eggs (well beaten)	1 pound raisins (3 cups ground)
9 ½ cups sifted flour	1 pint milk
1 tablespoons baking soda	Lemon extract, flavored to taste

There are no mixing directions with this recipe. I just beat together the shortening, sugar, molasses, and the 4 eggs; sift the flour, soda, and baking powder together and set it aside. Then, I emptied the shortening, sugar, molasses and eggs mixture into a very large bowl. Mix well. Next, I added the coconut, pecans, and raisins. On top of that, I added the flour mixture along with the pint of milk and lemon extract. Finally, I dug into the dough with both hands and kneaded it until I was satisfied that everything was mixed together. Shape into balls and roll in sugar. Bake at 375 degrees for 10 min.

A very young Mae Durden with her pre-school Companion Center students enjoying refreshment time with Ship Leyte cookies. On Mae's lap is new Durden son, Roger, born in 1962.

Christmas Cookies to Decorate*
by Grandma Sophie Durden

The following recipe has been used by the Durden family for at least forty-three years. Grandma always decorated these cookies for my three sons. They were not only delicious but pretty too. I never could accomplish or match her neat presentations. Sophie had much more patience than I will ever have.

3 cups all purpose flour	2 eggs
1 teaspoon baking powder	1 1/2 teaspoons vanilla
3/4 teaspoon salt	1 tablespoon milk
1 1/2 cups sugar	

Sift flour, measure after sifting. Add baking powder and salt. Sift again.

Cream shortening and sugar together until light and fluffy. Add eggs one at a time, beating well each time. Stir in vanilla and milk. Add dry ingredients and mix well until well blended.

Wrap dough in waxed paper and chill about 2 hours or overnight.

On a lightly floured board, roll dough 1/8" thick. Cut out in your choice of shapes. Bake on greased cookie sheet in moderate oven, about 375 degrees for 8 to 10 minutes. Cool thoroughly on rack. Icing to decorate.

Sugarplums

*Easy, delicious, and after aging
in the refrigerator, super wonderful.*

Place one cup of each in food processor: dried dates and golden raisins.

Add 1/2 cup each: dried cherries, apricots, white chocolate chips and pecans. Pulse mixer several times to chop coarsely.

Add 1 tablespoon orange juice and pulse until mixture holds together.

Form into 1 inch balls and roll in 1/3 cup Turbinado (raw sugar). Cover and refrigerate until firm. Makes 36 Sugarplums. Freezes well.

On Making Gingerbread Houses

At the beginning I was a very conservative builder. After a while the buildings became more elaborate. Even my macho husband got caught up in the excitement and offered to enhance the interiors with tiny electric lights with an outside on and off switch. We only did this at Christmas time. I also decorated the interiors with miniature Christmas trees, furniture and stuff. For Easter, we made Bunny Barns with candy Easter eggs and miniature bunnies. (A basic heavy freeform cardboard decorated platform should present your creation and should be half again as wide as the house is tall to give your design its best presentation.) **BE CREATIVE AND HAVE FUN!**

Some of these gingerbread creations were used as elementary school library reading contest prizes. One year, the owner of one of our local beauty shops asked me to build two gingerbread houses for prizes for a Christmas contest that she was presenting. When I charged her only the actual cost of the creations, she quickly decided to make the contest a one-time event. So, take warning, this can become an expensive adventure.

More words of advice: When building a gingerbread house, plan to take several days. 1st) Build your cardboard house; 2nd) Bake and attach the gingerbread siding; and finally, 3rd) Decorate your roof and etc. with various candies and icings.

Most important, mix gingerbread dough the day before your planned construction. Also, be prepared to have a big mess to clean up after your project is done. One tends to get caught up in the exciting creative process and neatness gets all over the kitchen and all over your hair.

Gingerbread House Dough

1 cup shortening	5 cups all-purpose flour
1 cup white sugar	1¹/₂ teaspoons soda
1 egg	1¹/₂ teaspoons salt
1 cup molasses	2-3 teaspoons ginger
*2 tablespoons apple cider	and cinnamon
vinegar	1 teaspoon cloves

Mix first 5 ingredients thoroughly. Add dry ingredients. Knead into a ball. Refrigerate overnight. Roll out ¹/₄ inch thick *on the baking sheet* and cut out in your pattern. Pick away the off-fall and knead it back into the dough to use again. Bake on greased sheet. 10 minutes at 350 degrees.

Important as it keeps the gingerbread dough at the exact size as your pattern, making for easy construction onto the cardboard house. Baked gingerbread does not trim well.

MORTAR MIX: Mix powdered sugar with water until easy to spread.

Two of twelve gingerbread houses built in my kitchen for either grandchildren or library contest prizes. In the top photo, Chisom Durden admires a gingerbread house. In the bottom photo, Kristen Durden reacts to her gingerbread merry-go-round.

First place winner of gingerbread house in a library contest

Library children and ginerbread houses are a perfect match.

Second place winner is a Gingerbread Mill with water wheel in a library contest.

Snickerdoodles

1 1/2 cups sugar	2 teaspoons cream of tartar
1/2 cup margarine	1 teaspoon baking soda
1/2 cup shortening	1/4 teaspoon salt
2 eggs	3 tablespoon sugar
2 3/4 cups all-purpose sifted flour	1 tablespoon ground cinnamon

Mix the 1 1/2 cups sugar, margarine, shortening and eggs in large bowl. Sift in flour, cream of tartar, baking soda and salt.

In a separate bowl, mix together 3 tablespoons sugar and 1 tablespoon cinnamon.

Shape dough by rounded teaspoonfuls into balls and roll into sugar/cinnamon and place on ungreased cookie sheet 2 inches apart.

Bake at 400 degrees for 8 to 10 minutes or until set. Immediately remove from cookie sheet and cool on a wire rack. Makes 5 dozen cookies.

Molasses Cookies *by Diane Hutton*
These are especially good when served with orange sherbet drizzled with orange liqueur.

1 cup packed brown sugar	1/4 teaspoon salt
1/2 cup vegetable shortening	2 teaspoons baking soda
1/2 cup molasses	1 teaspoon ground cinnamon
1 large egg	1/2 teaspoon ground cloves
2 1/4 cups all-purpose flour	1/2 teaspoon ground ginger

Combine brown sugar and shortening in a large bowl, beating with a mixer at medium speed until light and fluffy. Add molasses and egg; beat well. Lightly spoon flour into dry measuring cups. Combine flour and next 5 ingredients (through salt), stirring with a whisk. Add flour mixture to sugar mixture; beat at low speed just until blended. Cover and freeze 1 hour.

Preheat oven to 375 degrees.

Place water in a small bowl and sugar in another small bowl. Lightly coat hands with cooking spray. Shape dough into 1 inch balls. Dip one side of each ball in water, dip wet side in sugar. Place balls sugar side up, 1 inch apart on baking sheets coated with cooking spray. Bake at 375 degrees for 8 minutes. Remove from pans; cool on wire racks. Yield 4 dozen cookies.

Cookie Recipe Makes History

Certain recipes become famous, spread like wildfire, and everyone who is a cook makes them. According to Wikipedia, the free encyclopedia: The chocolate chip cookie was accidentally developed by Ruth Wakefield in 1930. She owned the Toll House Inn, in Whitman, Massachusetts. The restaurant's popularity was not just due to its home-cooked style meals; her policy was to give diners a whole extra helping of their entrées to take home plus a serving of her homemade cookies for dessert. Her cookbook, *Toll House—Tried and True Recipes*, was published in 1936 by M. Barrows & Company, New York. It included the recipe "Toll House Chocolate Crunch Cookie," which rapidly became a favorite to be baked in American homes.

During WWII, GIs from Massachusetts who were stationed overseas shared the cookies they received in care packages from back home with soldiers from other parts of the United States. Soon, hundreds of GIs were writing home asking their families to send them some Toll House Cookies. Wakefield was soon inundated with letters from around the world asking for her recipe. Thus began the nation-wide craze for the chocolate chip cookie.

To honor the cookie's creation in the state, it was proposed by a third-grade class from Somerset, Massachusetts, and on July 9, 1997, Massachusetts designated the chocolate chip cookie as the Official State Cookie.

"C is for Cookie, that's good enough for me."
—COOKIE MONSTER

Original Toll House Cookie

2 ¼ cups all-purpose flour (I add about ½+ cup more flour)
1 teaspoon baking soda
1 teaspoon salt
1 cup (2 sticks) butter, softened
¾ cup granulated sugar
¾ packed brown sugar

1 teaspoon vanilla
2 large eggs
2 cups (12-oz. pkg.) Nestlé's Toll House Semi-Sweet Chocolate Morsels
1 cup chopped nuts

Combine flour, baking soda, and salt in small bowl. Beat butter, granulated sugar, brown sugar, and vanilla in large mixer bowl, until creamy. Add eggs, one at a time, beating well after each addition. Beat in flour mixture. Stir in morsels and nuts. Drop by rounded tablespoon onto ungreased baking sheets.

Bake at 375 degrees, 9 to 11 minutes. Makes about 60 cookies.

A plate of Toll House cookies. Yum, yum!

This cookie marathon chapter ends with the one recipe that demands Bill Nelson's picture be alongside. Bill and I were married in August 1997. We'd just returned from our honeymoon and it was lunchtime. When I asked what to fix for his lunch, without hesitation he said, "I always have two pieces of bread. Cut off a third of the two slices. On the two-thirds part, I put a little mayo and a slice of cheese and a slice of lunchmeat and it goes into the toaster. On the remaining one-third part, I have peanut butter and jelly. I also usually have seven baby carrots, one-half apple cut into slices, one cookie, and a glass of tea." Bill added that he has had this lunch everyday for almost all of his life. "Yes Sir! Peanut butter is food fit for the gods!"

Ah, yes! The man has a *passion* for peanut butter!

Ultimate Peanut Butter Cookies

³/₄ cup creamy peanut butter   1 tablespoon vanilla
¹/₂ cup butter flavored Crisco   1 egg
   shortening   1³/₄ cups flour
1¹/₄ cups firmly packed   ³/₄ teaspoon salt
   light brown sugar   ³/₄ teaspoon baking soda
3 tablespoons milk

Heat oven to 375 degrees.

Combine Crisco, light brown sugar, milk, and vanilla in large bowl. Beat at medium speed of electric mixer until well blended. Add egg. Beat just until blended.

Combine flour, salt, and baking soda. Add to creamed mixture at low speed. Mix just until blended. Roll into small balls and place 2 inches apart onto ungreased baking sheet. Flatten slightly in crisscross pattern with tines of fork.

Bake at 375 for 7 to 8 minutes or until set and just beginning to brown. Cool 2 minutes on baking sheet. Remove cookies to cool completely. Makes about 3 dozen cookies. Freezes well.

> "Who would guess that a peanut butter and bacon sandwich is so good it will bring tears to your eyes? It does. Add lettuce, and you have a complete meal, with every known daily nutrient needed by the average 200 pound man."
>
> —ROGER WELSCH, *Diggin' In and Piggin' Out* (1997)

CHAPTER TWO

Bars & Candy

TURN TO THE BAR WHEN COOKIES ARE GONE
(I love bars. Yes, those too! These bars have
become favorites throughout the years.)

Bisquit Bars
From a morning Kaffee Klatch with Coleen Bohnert

1 box (16 oz.) box
  light brown sugar
4 eggs

2 tablespoons vanilla
2 cups Bisquick
1 cup pecans, chopped

Dump it all into a mixer bowl and mix well. Pour into a 9"x 9" pan and bake at 350 degrees for 30 minutes. Will look like a failure but tastes yummy!

Magic Cookie Bars

$^1/_2$ cup butter
$1^1/_2$ cups graham cracker
  crumbs or chocolate
  cookie crumbs
1 (14 oz.) sweetened
  condensed milk

2 cups semi-sweet
  chocolate chips
$1^1/_3$ cups flaked coconut
1 cup chopped nuts

Preheat oven to 350 degrees (325 if glass pan) Use a 13"×9" pan. Melt butter in oven. Sprinkle graham cracker crumbs over the butter. Pour condensed milk evenly over crumbs. Top with remaining ingredients. Press down firmly with fork. Bake 25 minutes or until lightly browned. Cool. Chill if desired. Cut into bars. Yummm!

Peanut Butter-Toffee Cheesecake Brownies
The 44th Pillsbury Bake-off Contest Finalist Recipe

1 box Pillsbury Chocolate
  Fudge Brownie Mix
1/2 cup vegetable oil
1/4 cup water
2 eggs
1 pkg. (8 oz.) cream cheese,
  softened

1 can sweetened
  condensed milk
1/2 cup creamy peanut butter
1 bag (8 oz.) milk chocolate
  toffee bits
1 cup milk chocolate baking chips
3 tablespoons whipping cream

Heat oven to 350 degrees. Lightly spray 13"×9" pan with cooking spray.

In a medium bowl, stir brownie mix, oil, water, and eggs 50 strokes with spoon. Spread batter in pan; set aside.

In a large bowl, beat cream cheese with electric mixer on medium speed until fluffy. Add milk and peanut butter; beat until smooth. Stir in 1 cup of the toffee bits. Spoon mixture over batter; spread evenly.

Bake 30 to 40 minutes or until cheesecake layer is set and edges are light golden brown. Cool on cooling rack 30 minutes. Refrigerate for 40 minutes.

In a small microwaveable bowl, microwave chocolate chips and cream uncovered on high 40 to 60 seconds or until chips are melted; stir until smooth. Spread over cheesecake layer. Sprinkle with remaining toffee bits. Cool completely. Store covered in refrigerator. Makes 36 bars.

Bourbon Balls

2 1/2 cups vanilla wafer crumbs
2 tablespoon cocoa
1 cup powdered sugar
1 cup finely chopped pecans

2 tablespoons light corn syrup
1/4 cup bourbon
Extra powdered sugar

Combine all ingredients, except extra powdered sugar. Roll into balls, then roll balls in extra powdered sugar. Makes 4 dozen. Rum or brandy may be used instead of bourbon. (They are best after sitting for a couple of days.) Can be frozen.

Strawberry Cheesecake Bars

1 cup graham cracker crumbs
3 tablespoons sugar
3 tablespoons butter, melted
5 pkgs. (8 oz. each) Philadelphia
   Cream Cheese, softened
1 cup sugar

3 tablespoons flour
1 tablespoon vanilla
1 cup sour cream
4 eggs
$1/3$ cup Smucker's strawberry
   jam

Preheat oven to 325 degrees. Line 13"×9" baking pan with foil, with ends of foil extending over sides of pan. Mix cracker crumbs, 3 tbsp. sugar and the butter; press firmly onto bottom of prepared pan. Bake 10 minutes.

Beat cream cheese, 1 cup sugar, the flour and vanilla in large bowl with electric mixer on medium speed until well blended. Add sour cream; mix well. Add eggs, one at a time, mixing on low speed after each addition just until blended. Pour over crust. Gently drop small spoonfuls of jam over batter; cut through batter several times with knife for swirl or marble effect. Bake 40 minutes or until center is almost set. Cool completely. Refrigerate at least 4 hours or overnight is best. Lift cheesecake from pan using foil overhang as handles. Cut into 16 bars to serve.

Even black and white photography cannot take away the appeal of this dessert bar.

Frosted Pineapple Supremes

1³/₄ cups sugar
2 cups flour
¹/₂ teaspoon baking soda
¹/₂ teaspoon salt
¹/₂ cup vegetable oil

2 eggs, beaten
2 cans(8 oz.) crushed pineapple
  including juice (divided use)
2 teaspoons vanilla
1 teaspoon lemon extract

Preheat oven to 325 degrees. Measure out 2 tablespoon crushed pineapple for frosting and set aside.

Combine sugar, flour, baking soda, and salt in a mixing bowl. Add vegetable oil, eggs, pineapple, vanilla and lemon extracts. Mix thoroughly.

Pour batter into a well-greased and floured 17"×11" inch jelly roll pan. Bake 25 to 30 minutes or until pick inserted in center comes out clean. Remove from oven and immediately frost with Coco-nutty Cream Cheese Frosting.

Coco-Nutty Cream Cheese Frosting

¹/₄ cup butter
1 cream cheese (3 oz.), softened
3 cups sifted powdered sugar
1 teaspoon vanilla

2 tablespoons crushed pineapple
1 cup flaked coconut
¹/₂ cup chopped nuts

Beat butter and cream cheese together. Add sugar, vanilla, and pineapple. Beat until well blended and smooth. Stir in coconut and nuts.

Butterscotch Crunch

1 cup butterscotch chips
¹/₂ cup crunchy peanut butter

1 cup crispy rice cereal
1 cup dry roasted peanuts

In a large microwaveable bowl, combine chips and peanut butter. Microwave on high for 30 seconds, stir well. Continue to microwave on high for 30 seconds at a time until melted and combined. Add the crispy rice cereal and peanuts; mix well. Pour the mixture into an 8"×8" baking pan and refrigerate until firm. Cut into 25 squares.

Gigi's Oat and Chocolate Bars

BATTER:

1 cup butter, softened	2¹/₂ cups flour
2 cups firmly packed brown sugar	1 teaspoon salt
2 eggs	1 teaspoon baking soda
2 teaspoons vanilla	3 cups uncooked quick oats

Preheat oven to 350 degrees. Lightly grease a 13"×9" inch baking pan. Cream together butter and brown sugar. Add eggs and vanilla. Stir in flour, salt, and baking soda. Add oats, mix well. Press two-thirds of the batter into the pan.

FILLING:

1 (12 oz.) package semi-sweet chocolate chips	2 tablespoon butter
	1 teaspoon vanilla
1 (14 oz.) can sweetened condensed milk	¹/₂ teaspoon salt
	¹/₂ cups chopped pecans

Melt chocolate chips with milk, butter, vanilla and salt over medium heat, stirring constantly to avoid scorching. Remove from heat as soon as chocolate is melted. Pour over batter in baking pan. Sprinkle with pecans. Crumple remaining batter over filling. Bake 25 to 30 minutes or until golden brown. Cut into bars when cooled. Yield: 24 bars

Hello Dolly Bars

¹/₂ cup butter	1 cup chocolate chips
1¹/₂ cups graham cracker crumbs	1 cup chopped pecans
1¹/₂ cups flaked coconut	1 can sweetened condensed milk

Preheat oven to 350 degrees. Melt butter in a 9"×13" cake pan. Spread evenly over the bottom of the pan. Sprinkle graham cracker crumbs evenly over the melted butter. Spread coconut evenly over the graham cracker crumbs, then add a layer of chocolate chips, then a layer of chopped pecans. Drizzle sweetened condensed milk evenly over top. Return to oven and bake for about 25 minutes, until lightly browned on top. Cool completely and cut into bars.

Apple Crunch

6 large apples, peeled, cored
   and thinly sliced
$^1/_2$ cup sugar
$^1/_2$ teaspoon nutmeg or
   cinnamon

1 cup flour
1 cup brown sugar
$^1/_2$ cup butter

Preheat oven to 325 degrees. Grease 8"×8" baking pan. Spread apples in pan. Top with granulated sugar and sprinkle with the nutmeg or cinnamon. Mix together flour and brown sugar. Cut in butter using pastry cutter until mixture resembles coarse meal. Spread over apples. Bake 1 hour. Serve with ice cream or whipped cream. Serves 6 to 8.

Double Lemon Bars

CRUST:
$^1/_3$ cup butter, softened
$^1/_3$ cup sugar

1 cup flour

Heat oven to 350 degrees. Combine all crust ingredients in small mixer bowl. Beat at medium speed, scraping bowl often until well mixed and mixture resembles coarse crumbs. Press into greased 8"×9" square baking pan. Bake for 15 to 17 minutes or until edges are lightly browned.

FILLING:
$^3/_4$ cup sugar
2 tablespoons flour
$^1/_2$ teaspoon salt

2 tablespoons lemon juice
1 tablespoon lemon peel
2 eggs

Combine all filling ingredients in same mixer bowl. Beat at medium speed until well mixed. Pour filling over hot partially baked crust. Continue baking for 17 to 20 minutes or until top is light golden brown. Sprinkle with powered sugar, cool. Cut into bars. Yield: 20 bars.

For easy cutting, line pan with aluminum foil, leaving 1 inch overhanging at ends. Lightly grease foil. Bake as directed above. Lift out foil from pan and cut into bars.

Apple Annie's Lemon Squares
(a larger yield version)

BASE:

1 cup (2 sticks) butter, cut into bits	2 cups flour $1/2$ cup powdered sugar

Preheat oven to 350 degrees. Cream together flour, butter and powdered sugar. Press evenly into an ungreased 11"×15" jellyroll pan. Bake 20 minutes, just until edges are golden.

FILLING:

4 eggs	$1/4$ cup flour
2 cups sugar	1 teaspoon baking powder
4-6 tablespoons fresh lemon juice	Powdered sugar for garnish
1 tablespoon lemon rind	

In a mixing bowl, beat together eggs, sugar, lemon juice, lemon rind, flour, and baking powder. Pour over baked crust, return to oven, and bake 20 to 25 minutes. Remove from oven and let cool. Sift with powdered sugar and cut into 2-inch squares.

Key Lime Bars

$1^{1}/_{2}$ cups coconut cookie
   crumbs (about 17 cookies)
	1 can (14 oz.) sweetened
	   condensed milk

3 tablespoon butter, melted	$1/4$ cup lime juice
1 pkg. (8 oz.) cream cheese, softened	1 tablespoon grated lime peel

Heat oven to 350 degrees. Grease square pan 9"×9"×2".

Mix cookie crumbs and butter thoroughly with fork. Press evenly in bottom of pan and refrigerate while preparing cream cheese mixture.

Beat cream cheese in small bowl with electric mixer on medium speed until light and fluffy. Gradually beat in milk until smooth. Beat in lime juice and lime peel and a little green food color and spread over layer in pan.

Bake about 35 minutes or until center is set. Cool 30 minutes. Cover loosely and refrigerate at least 3 hours until chilled. Serves 36 bars. Store in refrigerator.

Key Lime Bars
(another version)

CRUST:

8 tablespoon (2 sticks)   1 cup flour
   unsalted butter, softened $^1/_4$ teaspoon salt
$^1/_4$ cup sugar

Preheat oven to 350 degrees. Line an 8"×8" inch baking pan with foil, leaving an overhand. Mist foil with cooking spray.

Using an electric mixer on medium high speed, beat butter and sugar until light. Beat in flour and salt. Press evenly over bottom of pan. Bake until firm and light golden 20-26 minutes. Cool slightly.

FILLING:

2 large eggs $^1/_3$ cup lime juice
1 large egg yolk   1 teaspoon lime zest
1 cup sugar   2 tablespoons flour

Using an electric mixer on medium speed, beat eggs, yolk, and sugar until smooth. Stir in lime juice and zest. Fold in flour.

Pour filling over crust, and bake until set 20 to 30 minutes Cool on a wire rack. Cover and refrigerate at least 1 hour or overnight. Use foil overhand to remove bars from pan to cut. Dust with confectioner's sugar just before serving.

Such a nice, cool dessert to serve on a hot summer day— or ANY day!

Cherry Nut Bars

2 cups flour
2 cups uncooked
   quick-cooking oatmeal
1 1/2 sugar
1 1/4 butter, melted

1 teaspoon soda
1/2 cup chopped pecans
1 cup miniature marshmallows
1 can (21 oz.) cherry pie filling

Heat oven to 350 degrees. Combine all ingredients except pie filling and marshmallows in a large bowl. Beat at low speed, scraping bowl often until mixture resembles coarse crumbs. Reserve 1 1/2 cups of this mixture for the topping. Press remaining mixture into ungreased 13×9" baking pan. Bake for 12-15 minutes or until lightly browned on edges.

Gently spoon pie filling evenly over hot partially baked crust; sprinkle with marshmallows. Next, sprinkle with reserved crumb mixture. Continue baking for 25-30 minutes or until lightly browned. Cool completely. Makes 36 bars.

Cherry Coconut Bars

CRUST:
1 cup flour
3 tablespoon powdered sugar

1/2 cup butter, softened

Preheat oven to 350 degrees. Combine flour, powdered sugar, and butter in a medium bowl. Mix well. Press into an 8"×8" inch square baking dish. Bake 20-25 minutes until lightly golden.

FILLING:
2 eggs, beaten
1 cup sugar
1/4 teaspoon baking powder
3/4 cup pecans
1/2 cup coconut

1/2 cup maraschino cherries,
   drained and quartered
1 teaspoon vanilla
1/4 teaspoon salt
1/4 cup flour

Combine all ingredients in a large bowl; mix well. Spoon on top of crust and spread evenly.

Bake 20-25 minutes, until golden brown. Cool completely on a wire rack before cutting. Makes 16 bars.

Strawberry Streusel Cheesecake Bars

CRUST:

2 pkgs. (7 oz.) Martha White   6 tablespoons cold butter
Strawberry Muffin Mix

Heat oven to 350 degrees and spray bottom and sides of a 10"×11" spring form pan with no-stick spray.

Combine muffin mix and butter in medium bowl. Cut in butter with pastry blender until mixture is crumbly. *Reserve 1+ ¹/₃ cups crumb mixture and place in refrigerator.* Press remaining crumbs into spring form bottom and partially up side of pan. Place pan on cookie sheet; bake 10 minutes.

FILLING:

2 pkgs. (8 oz.) cream cheese,   2 tablespoons flour
  softened   1 egg
¹/₂ cup sugar   1 teaspoon vanilla

Combine cream cheese, sugar, flour, egg, and vanilla in a large bowl. Beat with electric mixer on medium high for 2 minutes or until creamy and smooth. Spoon cream cheese mixture evenly over partially baked crust; spread gently.

TOPPING:

1 can (21 oz.) strawberry   ¹/₂ cup chopped pecans
  pie filling

Spoon pie filling evenly over cream cheese mixture. Sprinkle with reserved crumbs and chopped pecans. Bake 40 to 45 minutes longer or until light golden brown. Cool—best chilled overnight in refrigerator.

To serve, remove sides from spring form part, place on serving plate. Cut into wedges. Store in refrigerator.

> "Cooking is at once child's play and adult joy.
> And cooking done with care is an act of love."
> —CRAIG CLAIBORNE, *Kitchen Primer*

Banana Split Cheesecake Squares

2 cups crushed low-fat
  graham crackers
$^{1}/_{3}$ cup butter, melted
1 cup sugar, divided use
3 pkg. (8 oz.) Philadelphia
  Cream Cheese
1 teaspoon vanilla
$^{3}/_{4}$ cup egg product
  (Egg Beaters)

$^{1}/_{2}$ cup mashed banana
1 cup halved strawberries
1 banana, sliced, tossed with
  1 teaspoon lemon juice
1 can (8oz.) pineapple tidbits,
  drained

Mix crushed graham cracker crumbs, butter, and $^{1}/_{4}$ cup of the sugar. Press into bottom of 13"×9" baking pan.

Mix cream cheese, remaining $^{3}/_{4}$ cup sugar, and vanilla with electric mixer until well blended. Add egg product; mix until blended. Stir in mashed banana and pour into crust.

Bake at 350 degrees for 40 minutes or until center is almost set. Cool and refrigerate overnight. Top with strawberries, sliced banana, and pineapple. Sprinkle with nuts and drizzle with melted semi-sweet baking chocolate. Cut into 18 squares. 170 calories per square.

You put *how many* pecans on those brownies?

> "I figured if I was going to make the world a better place, I'd do it with cookies."
> —ANA PASCAL, *Stranger Than Fiction*

Black and White Brownies

1 pkg. (19-21 oz.) fudge
brownie mix
1 pkg. (10-12 oz.) white
baking pieces
1 cup semisweet
chocolate pieces
$^1/_2$ cup pecan pieces

$^1/_4$ cup butter, melted
3 tablespoons hot water
2 cups sifted powdered sugar
$^1/_4$ cup unsweetened
cocoa powder
1 teaspoon vanilla
$^3/_4$ cup pecan pieces

Preheat oven to 350 degrees. Grease the bottom of 13"×9" pan; set aside. Prepare brownie mix according to package directions. Stir in half of the white baking pieces, all of the semisweet chocolate pieces and the $^1/_2$ cup pecans. Spread batter in the prepared pan.

Bake about 30 minutes or until center is set. Sprinkle with the remaining white baking pieces, bake for 1 minute more. Cool completely in pan on a wire rack.

FROSTING:

In a small bowl combine melted butter and hot water. Stir in powdered sugar, cocoa powder, and vanilla. Beat by hand until smooth. Spoon over top of brownies.

Sprinkle with $^3/_4$ cup pecans. Cool about $1^1/_2$ hours or until frosting is set. Cut into 36 bars.

Martha Washington Chocolates

Melt $^1/_4$ butter
Add 1 can Eagle Brand milk
2 pounds powdered sugar

1 can coconut
1 quart pecans, chopped fine

Combine all ingredients. Roll into desired shapes, bars if desired, cover and place in refrigerator to chill at least 1 hour or overnight. (May be frozen until ready to dip).

DIPPING MIX:

2 packages semi-sweet chocolate   1 bar ($^1/_4$ pound) paraffin

Melt chocolate and paraffin together. Stick toothpick in each ball or individually shaped bar and dip in chocolate dipping mix. Place on waxed paper on a jellyroll pan. Chill again.

Chewy Chocolate Marble Bars

1 cup semisweet chocolate
  chips
²/₃ cup sweetened condensed
  milk
1 tablespoon butter
1¹/₂ cups light brown sugar,
  packed

³/₄ cup butter, melted
2 large eggs
1 teaspoon vanilla
2 cups Bisquick
1 cup uncooked old-fashioned
  oatmeal

Preheat oven to 350 degrees. In 4 cup glass measuring cup, combine chocolate chips, sweetened condensed milk, and 1 table-spoon butter. Microwave on high for 1 to 2 minutes, stirring after every 30 seconds. Stir until chocolate is melted. Set aside.

In a large mixing bowl, stir together brown sugar, ³/₄ cup butter, eggs and vanilla until smooth. Stir in Bisquick and oats until well combined. Spoon ²/₃ of the batter into a 9"×13" baking pan that has been coated with nonstick spray; press to flatten. Drop chocolate mixture by teaspoonfuls over batter. Drop teaspoonfuls of remaining batter over top of chocolate. Swirl together with tip of knife. Bake for 20 to 25 minutes or until light golden brown and center is almost set. Cool completely. 36 small bars.

Bon Bons

1 can Eagle Brand Milk
2 boxes powdered sugar
2 to 3¹/₂ oz. cans angel flake
  coconut

4 cups chopped pecans
1 teaspoon vanilla
¹/₂ cup butter
Pinch of salt

Combine all ingredients. Place in refrigerator to chill at least 1 hour (or overnight). Form into balls about 1-inch in diameter and place balls on a jelly roll pan. Chill again. (May be frozen until ready to coat). Coat with 2 packages German Sweet Chocolate and ¹/₄ pound paraffin melted in double boiler. Leave plain or press a pecan half on top. Makes approximately 50 Bon Bons.

> "Never eat more than you can lift."
> —MISS PIGGY

I believe it's
time for a
coffee break!

Glazed Apple Bars

¹/₂ cup butter, softened	2 cups flour
1¹/₂ cups packed light	1 teaspoon baking soda
brown sugar	1 medium apple, peeled
¹/₂ teaspoon salt	and chopped
¹/₂ teaspoon ground nutmeg	1 cup raisins
1 teaspoon ground cinnamon	1 cup chopped pecans
1 teaspoon ground cloves	¹/₄ cup 2% milk
1 egg	

Preheat oven to 400 degrees. Lightly grease a 15"×10" jelly roll pan.

Cream butter and brown sugar with a mixer at medium speed. Add salt, nutmeg, cinnamon, cloves, and egg. Beat until well blended. Set aside.

Combine 1 cup flour and baking soda in a bowl; add to butter mixture. Stir in apple, raisins, and pecans by hand. Add milk and remaining flour; mix well. Spread in prepared pan. Bake 10 to 15 minutes until brown. Cool 10 minutes.

GLAZE:

¹/₂ cups confectioner's sugar	¹/₄ teaspoon vanilla
2¹/₂ tablespoon warm milk	¹/₈ teaspoon salt
1 tablespoon butter	

Combine confectioner's sugar, milk, butter, vanilla, and salt in a bowl; mix well and spread over cooled bars and cut to serve. Makes 2 dozen bars.

German Chocolate Brownies

1 (4 oz.) package Baker's
  German Sweet chocolate
6 tablespoons butter
³/₄ cup sugar

2 eggs, beaten
1 teaspoon vanilla
³/₄ cup flour
¹/₂ cup pecans, chopped

Preheat oven to 350 degrees. Line bottom and side of 8"×8" pan with foil, with ends of foil extending over side of pan. Grease foil, set aside.

Melt chocolate and butter in a saucepan over medium heat stirring until chocolate is completely melted. Allow chocolate to cool.

In a large bowl, mix together sugar, eggs, and vanilla. Pour in the cooled chocolate; stir to combine. Gently stir in flour and pecans until well blended. Spread into prepared pan. Bake 25 minutes or until toothpick inserted comes out clean. Cool completely before frosting. While brownies bake, prepare coconut frosting.

Coconut Frosting

1 cup evaporated milk
1 cup sugar
3 egg yolks
1 stick butter

1 teaspoon vanilla
1¹/₂ cups coconut
1 cup pecans, chopped

In a large saucepan over medium heat, combine milk, sugar, egg yolks, butter, and vanilla. Cook, stirring frequently, until thickened, 10-12 minutes. Remove from heat and stir in vanilla, coconut, and pecans. Allow frosting to cool 10 minutes before spreading on brownies. Lift brownies from pan using foil overhang and smear with coconut frosting. Serve each with a dollop of Cool Whip or vanilla ice cream, and a cherry on top.

Make sure dessert is warm and the milk is cold!

Million Dollar Fudge
You can't fail. Makes 5 pounds of
extra rich soft and creamy fudge.

3 Hershey bars (5 oz. each,
  broken into a bowl)
2 pkgs. (6 oz. each) chocolate
  chips
1 jar marshmallow crème

1 tablespoon butter
1 teaspoon vanilla
4$\frac{1}{2}$ cups sugar
1 can evaporated milk
14-oz. pkg. shelled pecans

Mix chocolates, marshmallow crème, butter and vanilla. Set aside.
Bring sugar and milk to a boil and boil for 6 minutes. Pour over
chocolate mixture and beat until creamy. Add pecans. Place in a
shallow pan and cool. Cut into desired squares.

No-Bake Chocolate Kahlua Christmas Balls
(Instead of Kahlua, try Crème de Cacao or another liqueur)

1 cup semi-sweet chocolate
  chips
1 can (5 oz.) evaporated milk
1$\frac{1}{4}$ cups vanilla cookie crumbs
1$\frac{1}{4}$ cups ginger snap cookie
  crumbs

$\frac{1}{2}$ cup confectioner's sugar, sifted
$\frac{1}{2}$ cup finely chopped pecans
$\frac{1}{3}$ cup Kahlua liqueur
1 teaspoon vanilla
2 cups shredded coconut

Melt the chocolate chips in evaporated milk in a pan over low
heat, stirring constantly, until well blended. Remove from heat and
set aside to cool for 30 minutes.

Combine all remaining ingredients except the coconut. Stir into
the chocolate mixture, blending well. Shape the mixture into 1 to
1$\frac{1}{2}$ inch balls. (If the dough is too moist, add up to $\frac{1}{3}$ cup more
cookie crumbs.) Roll balls in coconut. Let air dry for 2 hours on
waxed paper. Transfer to an airtight container, store in refrigerator.
Makes about 4 dozen.

"I can't cook. I use a smoke alarm as a timer."
—CAROL SISKIND, AMERICAN COMEDIANNE

It is 1939 and our family is getting dressed for our annual pageant at the St. Peter's Lutheran Church in Doss, Texas. Come, the season is about to begin in our small rural community.

A Texas Hill Country
German Christmas Revisited

Little boys squirm in obviously uncomfortable starched white shirts, tucked half in, half out of bothersome itchy long pants; girls with bobbing Shirley Temple curls—clad in new red velvet and lace-collared dresses—some so shy and others so self-assured as they sing "Stille Nacht" and "O Tannenbaum" in German. Inside the old rock church, the walls resonate their innocent voices like honey dripping from flowers.

Next, dressed—well almost—in old faded adult blue and brown bathrobes, enter embarrassed pre-teens as shepherds and wise men. Mary and Joseph are seated beside a rough cedar crib and—if there is a newborn in the community—he would be the baby Jesus. Around the scene are white sheet-clad, various-sized angels with silver roping outlining wings and bouncing halos. Dramatic lines tell of the birth of Jesus with memorized selected Bible verses—in the German language.

Throughout, the usually staid German Lutheran congregation, all eyes are aglow with pride, and smiles are wide from doting parents, grandparents and relatives. They contribute their part too with joyous carol singing in German accompanied by the organist who laboriously belts out the music on a hand-pumped organ. Pity the poor older frantic teenager operating the pumping lever!

At the finale of the magical pageant, Sunday school teachers hand out brown paper Christmas bags containing an orange, an apple, and some candy—a rare sight during the depression.

In this Texas Hill Country farming community, Christmas officially begins with the St. Peter's Lutheran Sunday school Christmas Eve program. That one enchanted evening sets in motion all holiday activities.

Once home after the church program, in every house the children willingly sit by the closed living room door to

sing more Christmas carols, and they wait. Soon, satisfying a thrilling anticipation, they hear the click—the door
unlocked from the other side! Santa Claus is *In There*!
However, the children must sing at least one more song
before they may enter. Finally, Daddy returns from some
unknown chore just in time to enter along with his family!

All over the community, living rooms are unlocked
thusly on Christmas eve and a huge native cedar tree—
that most fathers have enhanced by inserting a branch
here and there to "fill out" the tree—now stands adorned
and decorated with iced cookies, shining ornaments, glis-
tening icicles, and either wax candles or (after 1942)
bright new electric lights. (Alas, that is, until one light
fails and all the rest go dark!) If candles, there is a bucket
of water discretely set nearby in case of fire.

No matter! Papa hands out the few unwrapped gifts,
one to each child. All are hand-made. Two years ago, the
little girl got a medium sized doll whose only talent is to
open and close her eyes. The following year the doll received new clothes. This year there is a new handcrafted
cradle and a hand-made quilt. If anyone has com-
plaints—they remain unspoken. The children know about
the shortage of money. Since parents do not dwell on it—
neither do the children. Santa Claus is living out the depression too!

St. Peter's Lutheran Church in Doss, Texas, as it appears today. It was built with limestone taken from my maternal grandfather Julius Lange's pasture, quarried by the men of the church, loaded onto wagons pulled by mules and horses (driven by my paternal grandfather Fred Hahn). The church was dedicated September 14, 1913. A hand-crafted altar crafted by the then Pastor Meyer in 1912 still serves as the focal point for worship today. An ornate pulpit was also crafted by Pastor Meyer—as well as the Baptismal font. Stained glass windows throughout the church enhance the interior and have recently been restored.

CHAPTER THREE

Pies

With my cookie and bar recipe marathon accomplished, and the Christmas theme is over . . . I must take a break. Let's explore pie baking as it was in my mother's farm kitchen in 1939.

We baked limited pies back then. We were a large family around the table and a pie does not feed many mouths. Consequently, most farm cooks baked only specialty pies—like fruit that was in season and harvested from our own trees and gardens. Since my father had a hankering for squash pie, we baked a lot of them. We used white scalloped squash. It took many for just one pie and they had to be peeled with a paring knife before cooking—taking up a lot of time. Subsequently, I remember when my mother discovered the Zucchini squash. She grew a bumper crop of those straight squash that year and she harvested only a few small tender ones to cook as vegetables. She left several on the vine to continue to grow until they were almost a foot long and then she'd glory in baking multiple squash pies.

Every farm also had several peach trees. Mostly the harvest was used to make jam and can fruit for the winter. Only then did we make peach cobblers. It was the family's pie of choice and there was celebration when one was served.

One pie we did bake regularly—year round—at least once a week, was with the by-product of churning our own cream for butter: buttermilk pie. On rare special occasions we even enhanced the top with a little bit of coconut.

And then, in the fall, came pecans. Depending on the abundance of the harvest, we made certain that we had enough pecans for all our planned Christmas cookies; only then did we bake pecan pie.

One kind of pie you did not see often in our home was meringue pie. It was the age before electric mixers. Perfect meringue required beating egg whites with sugar until stiff peaks formed. That was very time consuming and who could hand-whip and beat those suckers to meringue consistency?

Who? I later discovered such a woman. She became my mother-in-law!

Sophie Durden was not a large woman, in fact, she was very small boned. However, she had among her kitchen tools a large wire whip gadget. She would tuck a medium sized bowl under one arm and take that wire whip in the other hand—she had an ability that mesmerized me the first time—no—every time I saw her prepare meringue. When she beat those egg whites, she resembled a virtual high-speed whipping machine! Late in the '50s, my husband and I bought her a small hand-held electric beater. She used it for other things but she refused to use it to beat her meringue.

Sophie was an amazing cook—much to my chagrin when I first married her son. We later became good friends but I clearly remember during those early months she "showed me up" to be less experienced than she was in the kitchen. God Bless Sophie. She was, like my own mother, a true pioneer with a backbone made of iron and a will of the same quality. I am happy that her DNA exists in my three sons—they are better men because of it.

Even so, we will now talk pies. The following pages present recipes from my collection—pies that I have known and loved and declared "keepers." Enjoy!

There are so many yummy variations of buttermilk pie, you might want to try them all!

These are my four favorite Buttermilk Pie versions

Coconut Buttermilk Pie
by Charlotte Holmes' Cypress Creek Inn

2 cups sugar	1 teaspoon vanilla
1 stick margarine	$1/4$ teaspoon nutmeg
$1/3$ cup flour	1 cup coconut
3 eggs	1 cup buttermilk

Cream together sugar and margarine. Add flour and eggs, mix together. Mix in buttermilk, nutmeg and vanilla. Stir in coconut. Pour into 10" unbaked pie shell. Bake at 350 degrees for 1 hour and 10 minutes.

Buttermilk Pie

$3^3/4$ cups sugar	1 cup buttermilk
4 tablespoon flour	3 tablespoons butter, melted
6 eggs	2 unbaked pie shells
2 teaspoons vanilla	

Preheat oven to 450 degrees Combine sugar, flour, eggs, vanilla, buttermilk, and butter. Mix until well blended. Pour into pie shells and bake for 10 minutes. Reduce heat to 350 degrees and bake an additional 40-50 minutes until center is firm.

Buttermilk Chess Pie
by Jane Nelson

5 large eggs	6 tablespoons butter, melted
3 cups sugar	$1/4$ teaspoon nutmg
5 tablespoons flour	
$1^1/2$ cups buttermilk	2 teaspoons vanilla

Preheat oven to 350 degrees. Place eggs in a large mixing bowl, beat slightly. Add sugar and flour and beat on medium speed for 2 minutes until well blended. Add rest of ingredients, beat 3-4 minutes. Pour mixture into an unbaked 10" pie shell. Bake for one hour and perhaps 15 minutes longer until center is done.

Knock Your Socks Off Buttermilk Pie

2¼ cups sugar
4 eggs
2 teaspoons vanilla
3 tablespoons flour

¾ cup margarine, melted
1½ cups buttermilk
½ cup crushed graham crackers
¾ cup chopped pecans

Preheat oven to 325 degrees. In a large bowl, mix together sugar and eggs; add vanilla and flour. Stir in margarine and buttermilk—*do not beat*. Fold in the crushed graham crackers and pecans.

Pour into 2 nine-inch unbaked pie crusts, dividing mixture evenly between the two. Bake 45 minutes or until center is firm when tested with a knife.

Peach Cobbler

8-10 or more peaches,
  pitted and sliced
Sugar according to taste
Fruit Fresh
1 stick butter
1 cup flour
1 cup sugar

3 teaspoons baking powder
Pinch of salt
1 tablespoon vegetable oil
1 teaspoon vanilla
Milk
Sprinkle of cinnamon

Place pitted and sliced peaches in large bowl. Add sugar according to taste, Fruit Fresh, and set aside for 1 hour or longer.

Melt a stick of butter in the baking pan. Mix together flour, sugar, baking powder, salt, vegetable oil, and vanilla. Beat, adding just enough milk to make the consistency of cake batter. Pour onto the melted butter in a 9"×13" baking pan.

Pour peaches into the center of the cake batter and with a small fork or spatula push the peaches underneath the cake batter as much possible.

During the baking process, the batter will rise up and over the peaches. When that is done, sprinkle some sugar and cinnamon over the top of the baked batter.

Continue baking until cobbler is set. Serve with whipped cream or ice cream.

Gingered Peach Crisp

FILLING:

2¹/₂ to 3 pounds peaches (about 6 to 8 peaches) pitted and sliced
¹/₂ cup peach preserves

¹/₂ to 1 tablespoon peach liqueur, peach schnapps or peach brandy
¹/₈ teaspoon almond extract
2 tablespoon cornstarch

Preheat oven to 375 degrees. Spray an 11" x 9" baking dish with nonstick coating.

Combine all ingredients except cornstarch in a large bowl. Using your hands or potato masher, coarsely crush two handfuls peaches to release juice. Combine 3 tablespoons of the juice and cornstarch; mix with fingers until combined. Stir cornstarch mixture back into peach filling, distributing it thoroughly. Pour peach mixture into prepared pan.

TOPPING:

³/₄ cup oatmeal
²/₃ cup light brown sugar
³/₄ cup flour
¹/₄ teaspoon salt
¹/₂ teaspoon nutmeg
1 to 2 tablespoon crystallized ginger (optional)

¹/₃ cup cold butter, cut into dime-sized pieces
1 teaspoon vanilla
³/₄ cup chopped almonds

Combine first six ingredients (oatmeal through ginger). Cut in butter with pastry blender or your hands until crumbly. Stir in vanilla and almonds. Sprinkle oat mixture over peaches, distributing it evenly. Press down slightly with your hands. Bake 45 minutes or until top is brown and fruit bubbles. Serve warm. Makes 8 servings.

"Good moms let you lick the beaters ...
great moms turn them off first."
—ANONYMOUS

Country Peach Pie
My personal favorite

1 cup sugar	$^1/_3$ cup water
1$^1/_2$ tablespoons cornstarch	1 tablespoon
1$^1/_2$ tablespoons tapioca	3 cups sliced firm, ripe peaches
$^1/_2$ teaspoon cinnamon	

Cook the first six ingredients over slow heat until thickened. Add peach slices and cool. Pour into a nine-inch unbaked pie shell and top with a lattice or crumb topping. Sprinkle sugar and cinnamon on lattice or topping. Bake at 350 degrees for one hour or until bubbly and brown.

Peach Crumble

8 peaches, sliced	1 cup brown sugar
1 teaspoon lemon juice	$^1/_8$ teaspoon salt
1 cup flour	1 stick butter

Prepare sliced peaches tossed with fruit fresh and—depending on sweetness of the peaches—add some sugar. Set aside for an hour or longer. Then, melt 1 stick butter and pour and distribute evenly in a 9"×11" baking dish. Pour sliced peaches into the now buttered baking dish. Blend flour, brown sugar, and salt and cut in $^1/_2$ stick butter with fork and fingers and mix until consistency of coarse meal.

Sprinkle crumb mixture over the top of the peaches and sprinkle just a touch of cinnamon over the crumb mixture. Bake in moderately hot oven (375 degrees) for 30 minutes. Yum!

> While working for an organization that delivers lunches to elderly shut-ins, I used to take my four-year-old daughter on my afternoon rounds. She was unfailingly intrigued by the various appliances of old age, particularly the canes, walkers, and wheelchairs. One day I found her staring at a pair of false teeth soaking in a glass. As I braced myself for the inevitable barrage of questions, she merely turned and whispered, 'The tooth fairy will never believe this!'

Squash Pie

3 cups cooked, mashed squash
2 cups milk or cream
2 eggs
1 cup sugar

¹/₂ teaspoon cinnamon
1 teaspoon salt
Pinch of cloves
Shredded coconut (optional)

Mix above ingredients together and pour into an unbaked 9" shell. Bake at 350 degrees about 35 minutes or until knife inserted into center comes out clean. Serve without meringue.

Mission Trail Pecan Cobbler

7 eggs
2 cups white corn syrup
¹/₃ cup flour
3 tablespoon unsalted
  butter, melted

¹/₂ teaspoon salt
16 oz. sugar
1¹/₄ pounds pecan halves
  or chopped

Heat oven to 350 degrees. Spray a 9"×13" baking pan with nonstick cooking spray. Reform pie shells into rectangle shape in the prepared pan. Crimp edges in a decorative design.
Beat eggs in a large bowl using an electric mixer on medium speed for 1 minute. Add syrup and beat 1 more minute.
Combine flour and melted butter in a small bowl. Add flour/butter mixture to egg mixture. Stir in salt and sugar and beat with mixer for 2 minutes. Sprinkle pecans over pastry and pour egg mixture over pecans. Make sure pecans remain evenly distributed. Bake on center oven rack for 1 hour or until a knife inserted in center comes out clean. 12 servings.

Farmers' Markets are great places to buy fresh peaches. Who can resist that sun-warmed chin dribble!

Diet Pecan Pie

1 cup pecans	1 cup Splenda
3 eggs	1 teaspoon vanilla
1 cup sugar-free syrup	1 tablespoon molasses
2 tablespoon melted butter	

Preheat oven to 350 degrees. Place the pecans in one unbaked pie shell. Whisk all of the other ingredients together and pour over the pecans. Bake about 35 minutes until the filling is set in the middle and crust is lightly browned. Makes 10 servings with 110 calories per serving.

Pecan Pie

6 eggs	2 teaspoons vanilla
2 cups brown sugar	2-4 cups pecans,
1 cup light corn syrup	roughly chopped
1 cup butter, melted	

Preheat oven to 350 degrees. Whisk eggs briskly. Whisk in brown sugar, then corn syrup. Whisk in butter and vanilla. Stir in pecans. Divide between 2 nine-inch unbaked pie crusts. Bake for 45-50 minutes or until sharp knife inserted into center comes out clean.

1st Prize Pecan Pie

3 eggs	$^1/_2$ teaspoon vanilla
$^1/_2$ cup dark corn syrup	$^1/_2$ cup melted butter
$^1/_2$ cup light corn syrup	$^1/_2$ cup chopped pecans
$^1/_2$ cup sugar	$^1/_2$ cup pecan halves

Combine eggs, corn syrups, sugar, vanilla and butter in bowl. Beat thoroughly. Stir in chopped pecans. Pour mixture into 9" unbaked pie shell. Arrange pecan halves on top and bake at 375 degrees for 40 minutes or until filling is set.

> The state tree of Texas is the pecan tree.

Praline Chocolate Pecan Pie

2 eggs
1 cup sugar
$^1/_2$ cup melted butter
$^1/_4$ cup cornstarch

$^1/_4$ cup praline liqueur
1 cup chopped pecans
1 (6 oz.) package semisweet
  chocolate chips

Preheat oven to 350 degrees. Cream eggs and sugar; stir in butter, cornstarch, praline liqueur, pecans and chocolate chips. Mix well and pour into 1 unbaked 9 " deep-dish pie crust and bake until done, abut 45-50 minutes.

For serving, top with whipped cream or ice cream and drizzle liqueur over all. Makes 6-8 servings.

Fudge Pecan Pie

3 eggs, lightly beaten
1 cup light corn syrup
4 ounces German sweet
  chocolate, melted and cooled

$^1/_3$ cup sugar
2 tablespoons melted butter
1 teaspoon vanilla
$1^1/_2$ cups pecan halves

Preheat oven to 350 degrees. Combine eggs, corn syrup, melted chocolate, sugar, butter, and vanilla and mix well. Add pecans and pour into one 9" unbaked pie shell. Bake until set about 50-60 minutes. Cool well before slicing.

Smucker's Caramel Pecan Pie

3 eggs
$^2/_3$ cup sugar
$^1/_4$ cup butter, melted

1 (12 oz.) Smucker's
  caramel topping
$1^1/_2$ cup pecan halves

In mixing bowl, beat eggs slightly with fork. Add sugar and stir until dissolved. Stir in butter and Smucker's caramel topping. Mix well. Stir in pecan halves and pour filling into 1 unbaked pie shell. Bake at 350 degrees for 45 minutes or until knife inserted into the center comes out clean. Cool thoroughly on rack before serving. 8 servings.

Chocolate Pecan Torte

CRUST:

2 cups Oreo chocolate
  cookie crumbs

$^{1}/_{2}$ cup (1 stick) butter, melted
1 cup pecan pieces

Mix cookie crumbs and butter and press firmly onto bottom of a 9" spring-form pan. Sprinkle pecans pieces over crust.

PRALINE NUT LAYER:

$1^{1}/_{2}$ cups (3 sticks) butter

1 cup firmly packed brown sugar

Place butter and brown sugar in saucepan; cook over medium heat until mixture comes to boil. Boil 2-4 minutes or until thickened, stirring constantly. Pour over pecans; cool slightly then cover and freeze 3 hours until set.

CREAM CHEESE LAYER

2 packages (8 oz.) cream
  cheese, softened

$^{1}/_{2}$ cup powdered sugar
$^{1}/_{3}$ cup firmly packed brown sugar

Beat cream cheese, powdered sugar and brown sugar with electric mixer on medium speed until light and fluffy. Spread over praline nut layer. Refrigerate until chilled.

CHOCOLATE GANACHE

4 squares semi-sweet
  baking chocolate

$^{1}/_{3}$ cup whipping cream

Melt chocolate with whipping cream in small heavy saucepan; cook on very low heat just until chocolate is melted, stirring frequently. Remove from heat; cool completely. Spread chocolate mixture over cream cheese layer. Refrigerate at least 2 hours—best overnight—before serving.

Makes 16 servings. For easier cutting, rinse knife in hot water, a wet knife will slice through this dessert easier and prevent the layers from sticking to the knife.

"Too much of a good thing can be wonderful."
—MAE WEST

Chocolate Silk Pie

1 cup semi-sweet
   chocolate chips
$^1/_2$ (1 stick) butter
1 tablespoon unsweetened
   cocoa powder

1 cup sugar
1 pinch salt
3 eggs
$^2/_3$ cup evaporated milk
1 teaspoon vanilla

Preheat oven to 350 degrees. In a large microwave safe bowl, melt chocolate chips and butter at 50% power for 2 minutes or until butter is melted. Stir until smooth. Whisk in sugar, cocoa powder, salt, eggs, evaporated milk, and vanilla extract. Whisk until well blended.

Pour mixture into 9" unbaked pie shell. Bake 30 minutes or until filling has puffed and center still wiggles. Cool completely. Refrigerate until ready to serve. Garnish with whipped cream and chocolate shavings. Serves 8.

Creamy French Silk Pie

$^1/_4$ cup sugar
3 tablespoons cornstarch
$1^1/_2$ cup milk
1 teaspoon vanilla

1 cup semi-sweet
   chocolate chips
2 cups whipping cream
2 tablespoon powdered sugar

In a medium saucepan, combine sugar and cornstarch; blend well. Gradually add milk, cooking over medium heat until mixture boils, stirring constantly. Add vanilla and chocolate chips to milk mixture; cook until melted and smooth, stirring constantly. Pour into small bowl; cover surface with plastic wrap. Cool one hour or until completely cool.

In a large bowl, combine whipping cream and powdered sugar; beat until soft peaks form. Reserve $2^1/_2$ cups of whipping cream for topping. Beat cool chocolate mixture at medium speed until light and fluffy, about 1 minute, in a large bowl. Fold chocolate mixture into whipped cream until blended. Spoon into cooled 9" baked pie shell. Top with reserved whipped cream. Refrigerate 2 to 3 hours or until set. If desired top with chocolate curls. Store in refrigerator. 10 servings.

Velvety Chocolate Cream Pie

3/4 cup sugar
1/3 cup cocoa
1/3 cup cornstarch
1/4 teaspoon salt
3 eggs, beaten

3 cups milk
3/4 cup semi-sweet
    chocolate chips
3 tablespoons butter
2 teaspoons vanilla

Stir together sugar, cocoa, cornstarch, and salt in medium saucepan. Combine eggs and milk; gradually stir into sugar mixture, blending well. Cook over medium heat, stirring constantly with wire whisk, just until mixture comes to a boil. Remove from heat. Add chocolate chips, butter and vanilla. Stir until chips and butter are melted and the mixture is smooth.

Pour into prepared 9" pie crust baked and cooled. Immediately press plastic wrap onto pie surface. Refrigerate 3 to 4 hours until firm. Garnish with whipped topping and chocolate chips. Serves 8.

Black Forest Pie

1 graham pie crust
1 package (8-oz) cream
    cheese, softened
1/4 cup sugar
1/4 cup cocoa

1 egg
1/4 teaspoon almond extract
1 cup Cool Whip
1 can (21-oz) cherry pie filling

Preheat oven to 350 degrees. Beat cream cheese until fluffy; add sugar and cocoa, mix well. Add egg and almond extract. With a spatula, scrape filling into crust and spread evenly. Bake 35 minutes. Cool and refrigerate. Just before serving, top with Cool Whip and cherry pie filling.

"The two biggest sellers in any bookstore are the cookbooks and the diet books. The cookbooks tell you how to prepare the food, and the diet books tell you how not to eat any of it.."

—ANDY ROONEY

Black Forest Brownie Pecan Pie

1 cup Karo light or dark corn syrup	4 eggs, slightly beaten
1/2 cup sugar	1 teaspoon vanilla
1/8 teaspoon salt	1 cup pecans, chopped
4 oz. semi-sweet baking chocolate, broken	1 graham cracker crust
3 tablespoons butter	1 can (21-oz) cherry pie filling
	Whipped cream, optional

Combine corn syrup, sugar, and salt in a small saucepan. Bring mixture to a boil over medium heat, stirring until sugar is dissolved. Boil for 2 minutes and remove from heat. Add chocolate and butter to syrup mixture, stirring until chocolate is melted and mixture is smooth. Let cool for 5 minutes. Pour chocolate mixture slowly over eggs, stirring constantly. Add vanilla and pecans, mix well.

Place pie crust on a baking sheet. Pour mixture into crust. Bake in a 350 degree oven for 35 minutes, or until center of pie is slightly puffed; cool at least 1 hour. To serve, top each slice of pie with 1/4 cup cherry pie filling and a dollop of whipped cream, if desired. Serves 10.

Black Forest
Pie. Oh, my!

Ultimate Turtle Cheesecake

2 cups Oreo cookie crumbs	3 (8-oz.) packages cream
1 cup finely chopped	cheese, softened
pecans, divided use	3/4 cup sugar
6 tablespoon butter, melted	3 eggs
1 (14-oz.) package caramels	2 squares semi-sweet
1/2 cup milk	baking chocolate
1 tablespoon vanilla	

Mix crumbs, 1/2 cup of pecans, and all of butter; press onto the bottom and two inches up the side of 9" spring form pan. Place caramels in milk in small microwaveable bowl. Microwave on high 3 minutes or until caramels are melted, stirring after each minute. Pour 1/2 of the caramel mixture into crust. Refrigerate for 10 minutes. Cover and reserve remaining caramel mixture in refrigerator for later use.

Beat vanilla, cream cheese, and sugar with mixer on medium speed until well blended. Add eggs, 1 at a time, mixing on low speed after each addition, just until blended. Pour over caramel mixture in crust. Bake at 300 degrees for 60-70 minutes or until center is almost set. Refrigerate 4 hours or overnight.

Run knife around side of pan to loosen cake before removing side of pan. Microwave reserved caramel mixture for 15 seconds just before serving; drizzle over cheesecake. Sprinkle with remaining 1/2 cup pecans. Melt chocolate as directed on package and drizzle over cheese cake. Store in refrigerator. Serves 16.

Nothing says American like apple pie!

Perfect Apple Pie

6 cups thinly sliced and peeled	$^3/_4$ teaspoon cinnamon
Granny Smith apples	$^1/_4$ teaspoon salt
$^3/_4$ cup sugar	$^1/_8$ teaspoon nutmeg
2 tablespoon flour	1 tablespoon lemon juice

Preheat oven to 425 degrees. Combine sugar, spices, and salt and mix well. Add lemon juice and apples, toss gently to mix. Spoon into unbaked crust-lined pan. Top with either second pie crust or lattice work and seal edges. Protect edges all around with foil. Bake 40-45 minutes or until apples are tender and crust is golden brown. 8 servings.

Dutch Apple Pie

6 cups thinly sliced	1 teaspoons cinnamon
McIntosh apples	$^1/_2$ teaspoon nutmeg
1 cup sugar	$^1/_4$ teaspoon salt
$^1/_3$ cup flour	4 tablespoons heavy cream

Preheat oven to 425 degrees. Toss apples, sugar, flour, cinnamon, nutmeg, and salt together in a large bowl. Place into prepared unbaked crust. Pour the cream over it.

TOPPING:

$^1/_2$ cup butter	2 tablespoons flour
1 cup brown sugar	$^1/_2$ teaspoon cinnamon
$^1/_2$ cup chopped pecans	

Mix butter, brown sugar, pecans, flour, and cinnamon together until evenly blended. Spread evenly over the apple filling. Bake for 40-45 minutes. If crumb topping becomes overly brown, cover the pie with foil for the last 15 minutes of baking. Drizzle a bit of caramel sauce on top.

"No man can be a patriot on an empty stomach."
—WILLIAM COWPER BRANN, *The Iconoclast*

French Apple Pie

6 cups thinly sliced
  tart apples, peeled
1 cup white sugar
$^1/_4$ cup cornstarch

$^1/_2$ teaspoon nutmeg
$^1/_4$ teaspoon cinnamon
Pinch of salt

Preheat oven to 350 degrees. Mix sugar, cornstarch, nutmeg, cinnamon and salt into bowl. Stir in apples and pour into unbaked pie shell.

TOPPING:
1 cup flour
$^1/_2$ cup butter

$^1/_2$ cup brown sugar

Mix flour and butter with fork until crumbly. Add brown sugar and toss gently until crumbly. Distribute topping evenly on pie filling and bake $1^1/_2$ hours. Cover pie with foil for the final 10 minutes of baking. Tastes best when served warm.

Apple Dumpling Pie

CRUST:
$1^1/_2$ cups flour
$1^1/_2$ tablespoons sugar
1 teaspoon salt

$^1/_2$ cup cooking oil
2 tablespoons milk

Preheat oven to 425 degrees. Combine flour, sugar, salt, oil, and milk and press into an 8" deep-dish pie pan.

FILLING:
8 cups thinly sliced, peeled
  tart baking apples
1 cup sugar

2 tablespoons flour
3 tablespoons butter

Toss apples in sugar and flour, place in pie crust, and dot with the butter.

TOPPING:
1 cup flour
$^1/_2$ cup sugar

$^1/_2$ cup butter

Combine flour and sugar. Cut in butter until mixture resembles meal. Spread evenly over apples. Cover pie lightly with foil and bake 40-50 minutes.

Lemon Meringue Pie

1 cup sugar
$^1/_4$ cup cornstarch
1$^1/_2$ cup cold water
3 egg yolks, slightly beaten
Grated rind 1 lemon

$^1/_4$ cup lemon juice
1 tablespoon butter
3 egg whites
$^1/_3$ cup sugar

Preheat oven 350 degrees. In medium saucepan combine sugar and cornstarch. Gradually stir in water until smooth. Stir in egg yolks. Stirring constantly, bring to boil over medium heat and boil one minute. Remove from heat. Stir in next 3 ingredients. Spoon hot filling into baked 9" pie shell.

In small bowl, with mixer at high speed, beat egg whites until foamy. Gradually beat in $^1/_3$ cup sugar. Continue beating until stiff peaks form. Spread meringue evenly over hot filling, sealing to edge of crust. Bake 15-20 minutes or until golden brown. Cool on wire rack; refrigerate.

Grandma Durden's Lemon Pie

During baking, the cornmeal rises
to the top to become the top crust.

2 cups sugar
1 tablespoon flour
1 tablespoon cornmeal
4 eggs, unbeaten

$^1/_4$ cup melted butter
$^1/_4$ cup milk
4 teaspoons grated lemon rind
$^1/_4$ cup lemon juice

Place sugar, flour and cornmeal in a bowl and toss lightly with a fork. Add eggs, butter, milk, lemon rind and lemon juice. Beat with mixer until smooth and thoroughly blended.

Pour into baked pie shell and bake at 350 degrees oven for 35-45 minutes or until top is golden brown. Cuts warm.

> "I was 32 when I started cooking; up until then, I just ate."
> —JULIA CHILD

Lemon Cloud Pie

1 cup sugar	4 oz. cream cheese, cubed,
3 tablespoon cornstarch	softened
1 cup water	1 teaspoon grated lemon peel
$^1/_3$ cup lemon juice	$^1/_2$ cup whipping cream
2 egg yolks, slightly beaten	

In medium saucepan, combine sugar and cornstarch; mix well. Stir in water, lemon juice, and egg yolks. Cook over medium heat until mixture boils and thickens, stirring constantly. Boil 1 minute. Add cream cheese and lemon peel, stirring until cream cheese is melted and mixture is smooth. Cool to room temperature.

In large bowl, beat $^1/_2$ cup whipping cream until soft peaks form; fold into lemon mixture. Spoon filling mixture evenly into cooled baked pie shell. Cover surface with plastic wrap; refrigerate for at least 6 hours—best overnight. Serve with dollop of whipped cream over each serving.

Coconut Cream Meringue Pie

This is Grandma Sophie Durden's recipe that was published in Texas Co-Op *magazine with my article about her in May 2003.*

4 cups milk	3 eggs, separated
$^1/_2$ cup cornstarch	1$^1/_2$ tablespoons butter
1$^1/_2$ cups sugar	1 teaspoon vanilla
$^1/_2$ teaspoons salt	1$^1/_2$ cups coconut

Preheat oven to 350 degrees. In a heavy 2 quart saucepan, heat 3 cups of milk over medium heat. While the milk is heating, combine cornstarch, sugar, and salt in a bowl and gradually add the remaining cup of milk. Beat egg yolks and gradually add to the mixture. Mix well.

When the other milk is hot, slowly add the egg yolk mixture to it, stirring constantly until very thick. Remove from heat and add butter, vanilla, and coconut.

Pour into baked pie crusts, top with meringue and sprinkle top with coconut. Bake until golden brown.

Lemon Meringue Pie—The Winner!

Bobby Allen always bragged that his lemon pie recipe was the best over all others. I challenged him and he brought me this recipe and dared me to make it and bring it to our Sunday School class next week. I did. He was correct. This does beat all others I've tasted!

FILLING:

5 level tablespoons corn
starch—plus just a little more
2 cups water
1 cup sugar
¹/₈ teaspoon salt

3 egg yolks, well beaten
2 tablespoons butter
5 tablespoons lemon juice
2 teaspoons zest

Mix cornstarch with ¹/₂ cup cold water; add sugar, salt, and remaining water. Blend in top of double boiler and cook over low heat, stirring constantly until thickened. Gradually pour hot mixture over beaten egg yolks and return to double boiler and cook 2 minutes longer. Add butter, lemon juice and rind. Set aside.

MERINGUE:

3 egg whites, room temperature
¹/₄ teaspoon cream of tartar

1 jar marshmallow crème

Beat egg whites on high speed until foamy. Add cream of tartar and beat until it holds stiff peaks. Fold the marshmallow crème in slowly until well mixed with meringue. Pile on the pie and seal to edges of baked pastry. Bake at 350 degrees—until lightly browned.

Look how high the meringue is on this lemon pie!

Coconut Cream Pie
(smaller/richer with coconut)

FILLING:

2 cups milk	4 tablespoons flour
3 egg yolks	1 teaspoon vanilla
1/2 cup sugar	2 cups shredded coconut

Heat the milk until it almost comes to a boil.

Meanwhile, whisk egg yolks and add sugar and flour to the yolks. Pour into the milk over heat and stir until it gets a pudding-like consistency. Stir in vanilla and coconut. Set aside.

MERINGUE:

3 egg whites	1/2 cup sugar
Pinch of salt	

Add salt to egg whites and beat with a mixer on high until stiff. Stir in 1/2 cup sugar a little at a time and continue beating until peaks form.

Fill baked pie crust with coconut mixture and spread evenly across the bottom. Dollop the meringue on top, bringing it to the edges of the crust to seal.

Bake at 325 degrees for about 20 minutes or until top turns a light brown.

Next to apple pie, coconut cream is the most requested pie in the U.S.

Station Cafe's Coconut Cream Pie

MERINGUE:

Place 3 egg whites in the bowl of an electric mixer and whip the whites until smooth and fluffy and peaks have formed. Do not over-beat—the egg whites should remain shiny. Set aside in refrigerator.

TOPPING:

Lightly sweetened whipped cream $^1/_4$ cup toasted coconut

Toast coconut in oven while crust is baking until golden brown or about 12 to 15 minutes.

FILLING:

$^3/_4$ cup sugar	$^1/_2$ cup whole milk or
2 tablespoons cornstarch	half and half
$^1/_4$ teaspoon salt	$^1/_4$ teaspoon vanilla
3 egg yolks	$^3/_4$ cup sweetened coconut
1 can (12 oz.) evaporated milk	

In a saucepan, whisk together sugar, cornstarch, and salt. Add the egg yolks, evaporated milk, whole milk, and vanilla to the saucepan. Whisk to blend the ingredients. Place over medium heat and whisk to pudding constantly to prevent the mixture from sticking on the bottom and scorching and to avoid lumps from forming as the custard begins to thicken. Be sure to get into the edges of the pan as well. Bring the mixture to a boil, stirring rapidly and let boil for about 2 minutes or until the custard is thick, about 7-8 minutes. It should look glossy, not chalky.

Remove from the heat and immediately fold in the egg whites with a rubber spatula. The egg whites should be evenly mixed throughout with no traces of egg white showing.

Lastly fold in the coconut. Pour the filling into a 9" cooled baked pie shell, cover loosely and chill until set.

Before serving, add whipped cream to the top and sprinkle with toasted coconut. 8 servings.

Jesse Durden

Banana Pudding Pie

CRUST:

1 (12-oz.) box vanilla wafers, divided use	½ cup butter, melted
	2 large bananas, sliced

Set aside 30 vanilla wafers; pulse remaining vanilla wafers in a food processor 8 to 10 times or until coarsely crushed. Yield should be about 2½ cups. Stir together crushed vanilla wafers and butter until blended. Firmly press on bottom, up sides, and onto lip of a 9" pie plate. Bake at 350 degrees for 10-12 minutes or until lightly browned. Remove to a wire rack and let cool 30 minutes or until completely cool. Arrange banana slices evenly over bottom of crust.

FILLING:

½ cup sugar	4 egg yolks
¾ cup flour	2 cups milk
2 large eggs	2 teaspoons vanilla

Whisk together first 5 ingredients in a heavy saucepan. Cook over medium low heat, whisking constantly, 8-10 minutes or until it reaches the thickness of chilled pudding. (Mixture will begin to bubble and will be thick enough to hold soft peaks when whisk is lifted.) Remove from heat and stir in vanilla. Use immediately.

Spread half of hot filling over pie crust with bananas; top with 20 whole vanilla wafers. Spread remaining hot filling over vanilla wafers. (Filling will be about ¼ inch higher than top edge of crust. That's okay.)

MERINGUE:

4 egg whites	Sugar, as needed

Beat egg whites at high speed with electric mixer until foamy. Add sugar, 1 tablespoon at a time, beating until stiff peaks form and sugar dissolves. Spread meringue evenly over hot filling, sealing the edges. Bake at 350 degrees 10-12 minutes or until golden brown.

Remove from oven and let cool 1 hour on a wire rack or until completely cool. Coarsely crush remaining vanilla wafers (10) and sprinkle evenly over top of pie. Chill 4 hours or overnight. Serves 8.

French Vanilla Banana Cream Pie

1 banana, sliced
1 graham cracker pie crust
2 cups cold milk

2 pkg. (4-serving size) Jell-O
 vanilla instant pudding
2 cups thawed Cool Whip

Place banana slices in crust. Pour milk into bowl. Add pudding. Beat with wire whisk 2 minutes. Gently stir in 1 cup Cool Whip; spoon into crust. Refrigerate at least 4 hours and top pie with remaining Cool Whip. Serves 8.

Key Lime Pie
Dockside Seafood Restaurant, Savannah, Georgia

Our waitress gave us Texans this recipe after she told us this was the best key lime pie ever. We tested and she was right!

4 oz. key lime juice
4 egg yolks

1 can sweetened
 condensed milk

Blend ingredients and pour into a heated 9" graham cracker shell. Bake at 325 degrees for 7-9 minutes. Chill, serve, and enjoy!

Key Lime Pie
Weight Watchers recipe

1 box (3 oz.) sugar free
 Lime Jell-O
1/4 cup boiling water
2 containers (8 oz. each)
 Key Lime flavored yogurt

1 container (8 oz.) fat free
 Cool Whip

Dissolve gelatin in boiling water. Cool with wire whisk and then whisk in the yogurt. With a wooden spoon, fold in the whipped topping and transfer mixture into the prepared 9" reduced fat graham cracker pie crust. Refrigerate—best overnight. 8 servings. (1 piece = 3 WW points.)

> "There is no love sincerer than the love of food."
> —GEORGE BERNARD SHAW

Traditional Pumpkin Pie

1 can (15 oz) pumpkin	1 teaspoon cinnamon
1 can (14 oz.) sweetened condensed milk (**not** evaporated milk)	$^1/_2$ teaspoon ginger
	$^1/_2$ teaspoon nutmeg
	$^1/_2$ teaspoon salt
2 eggs	

Preheat oven to 425 degrees. Whisk all ingredients until smooth. Pour into unbaked 9" pie crust. Bake 15 minutes. Reduce heat to 350 degrees and continue baking 35-40 minutes or until knife inserted 1 inch from crust comes out clean. Cool. Garnish as desired.

Pumpkin Cobbler

3 eggs	1 teaspoon ginger
1 can (15 oz.) pumpkin	1 tablespoon vanilla
1 can (12 oz.) evaporated milk	1 box (18.1 oz.) yellow cake mix
1 cup sugar	$1^1/_4$ cup butter, melted
$^1/_8$ teaspoon salt	1 cup chopped pecans
$1^1/_2$ teaspoons cinnamon	

Mix the first 8 ingredients together, pour into an ungreased 13"×9" baking pan. Sprinkle cake mix over the top; drizzle with melted butter. Bake at 350 degrees for 25 minutes; top with nuts and bake for additional 15 minutes. Makes 15-18 servings.

Pumpkin Pecan Pie
Grandma Sophie Durden's recipe

3 slightly beaten eggs	1 teaspoon vanilla
1 cup canned or mashed pumpkin	$^1/_2$ teaspoon cinnamon
1 cup sugar	$^1/_4$ teaspoon salt
$^1/_2$ cup dark corn syrup	1 cup chopped pecans

Combine eggs, pumpkin, sugar, corn syrup, vanilla, cinnamon, salt. Mix well and pour into unbaked 9" pastry shell. Top with the chopped pecans. Bake at 350 degrees about 40 minutes.

Southern Pecan Pumpkin Pie

FILLING:

1 can (15 oz.) pumpkin pie filling $^1/_2$ teaspoon ginger
1$^1/_2$ tablespoon bourbon   1 teaspoon cinnamon
2 eggs, slightly beaten $^1/_2$ teaspoon salt
$^3/_4$ cup packed dark brown sugar   1$^1/_2$ cups half and half cream

Preheat oven to 435 degrees. Mix pumpkin pie filling, bourbon, eggs, brown sugar, ginger, cinnamon and salt. Blend in half and half. Pour into 9" unbaked deep-dish pie shell and bake 10 minutes, then reduce heat to 350 degrees and bake for 50 minutes more or until knife inserted near center comes out clean. Cool completely before topping.

TOPPING:

2 tablespoons butter   1 cup (or more) pecan halves
$^1/_4$ cup brown sugar   Whipped cream
1 tablespoon bourbon

Combine butter and sugar in a saucepan. Heat, stirring until sugar is completely dissolved, then stir in bourbon. Add pecans and stir. Spoon around edges of pie. Do this $^1/_2$ hour before serving so glaze can cool. Top pie with whipped cream. 8 servings.

Coconut Pumpkin Pie

1$^3/_4$ cups pumpkin puree   1 teaspoon cinnamon
1$^1/_2$ coconut milk $^1/_2$ teaspoon ginger
2 eggs $^1/_4$ teaspoon cloves
$^1/_2$ teaspoon salt   Whipped cream, for garnish

Preheat oven to 425 degrees. In a large bowl, mix pumpkin puree, coconut milk and eggs. Add salt, cinnamon, ginger and cloves and stir until well combined. Pour mixture into unbaked 9-inch pie shell and bake for 15 minutes. Reduce heat to 350 degrees and continue to bake for 30 to 40 minutes. Top with whipped cream and serve at room temperature. 8 servings.

Pumpkin Swirl Cheesecake Pie
Interesting and different taste

2 cups finely crushed
  gingersnaps
1/2 cup finely chopped pecans
6 tablespoons butter, melted
3 pkgs. (8 oz. each) cream
  cheese, softened
1 cup sugar, divided use

1 teaspoon vanilla
3 eggs
1 can pumpkin
1 teaspoon cinnamon
1/4 teaspoon nutmeg
Dash of cloves

Mix gingersnap crumbs, pecans, and butter and press onto bottom and 2 inches up sides of 9-inch spring form pan.

Beat cream cheese, 3/4 cup sugar, and vanilla with electric mixer on medium speed until well blended. Add egg, one at a time, mixing on low speed after each addition just until blended. Reserve 1 1/2 cups of this plain batter.

Next, stir remaining 1/4 cup sugar, the pumpkin and spices onto remaining batter.

Spoon 1/2 of the pumpkin batter over crust, then top with spoonfuls of 1/2 of the reserved plain batter. Repeat layers and then cut through batters with knife several times for marble effect. Bake at 325 degrees for 55 minutes or until center is almost set. Loosen cake from sides of pan and cool before removing rim of pan. Refrigerate at least 4 hours or overnight. 12 servings.

Sweet Potato Pie

1 1/2 cups mashed
  sweet potatoes
2 eggs, beaten
1 2/3 cups sugar
3/4 cup evaporated milk

1/2 cup butter, melted
1/4 cup light corn syrup
3 tablespoons flour
1/4 teaspoon nutmeg
Pinch of salt

Preheat oven to 350 degrees. Mix together all ingredients in a large bowl until smooth. Pour into 9-inch unbaked pie shell and bake for 50-60 minutes. Serve with a dollop of whipped cream.

From My Collection of Unusual Special Pies—
A Lot of Work, But Worth It

Decadent Peanut Butter Pie

1 cup creamy peanut butter
8 oz cream cheese
  (at room temperature)
1/2 cup sugar
12 oz. container non-dairy
  whipped topping, divided use

1 jar (11.75 oz.) Smucker's
  hot fudge ice cream topping,
  divided use

In a medium bowl, beat together the peanut butter, cream cheese, and sugar. Gently fold in 3 cups whipped topping. Spoon mixture into the pie shell. Using a spatula, smooth mixture to edges of pie.

Reserving 2 tablespoons of the hot fudge topping, place the remaining hot fudge into microwave safe glass measuring cup. Microwave for 1 minute, stir, and spread the fudge over a prepared chocolate cookie pie crust to cover the peanut butter layer. Refrigerate until serving time. Just before serving, spread the remaining whipped topping over hot fudge layer, being careful not to mix the two layers.

TOP DRIZZLE:
2 tablespoons fudge topping   2 tablespoons peanut butter

Place the hot fudge topping into a cake decorator and drizzle over pie. Do the same with the peanut butter, going in the opposite direction of the chocolate.

Rancher's Pie

1 1/2 cups sugar
1 cup crushed pineapple
  (do not drain)
3 lightly beaten eggs

3 tablespoons flour
1 cup flaked coconut
3/4 stick butter

Preheat oven to 350 degrees. Stir together sugar, pineapple, eggs, flour, and coconut in a bowl. Melt butter and add. Mix well and pour filling into unbaked pie shell. Bake one hour or until filling is set and browned. Yum!

Cherry Cheese Pie

1 pkg. (8 oz.) cream cheese, softened	1/3 cup lemon concentrate
	1 teaspoon vanilla
1 can (14 oz.) sweetened condensed milk	1 or 2 cans cherry pie filling, chilled

In a large mixer bowl beat cream cheese until fluffy. Beat in sweetened condensed milk until smooth. Stir in lemon and vanilla and pour into 9" graham cracker crumb crust. Chill 3 hours or until set. Serve with the cherry pie filling spooned over the top.

Daiquiri Pie

1 package (3 1/2 oz.) lemon pudding and pie filling (do not use instant)	2 eggs
	1/2 cup good quality rum
1 package (3 oz.) Jell-O lime gelatin	Several drops of green food coloring, if desired
1/3 cup sugar	2 cups frozen whipped topping, thawed
2 1/2 cups water	

In a saucepan, combine pudding mix, gelatin, and sugar. Stir in 1/2 cup water and eggs; blend well. Add remaining water. Cook, stirring constantly, over medium heat until mixture comes to a full boil. Remove from heat. Stir in rum and green food coloring, if desired. Chill.

When thoroughly chilled, fold in whipped topping. Spoon into baked 9" graham cracker crumb pie crust and chill until firm. Before serving, garnish top with whipped cream and lime twist.

CHAPTER FOUR
Cakes

The art of baking *cakes* has a long colorful history. Egyptians and Greeks baked cakes called *plakous* by the Greeks. There are literally thousand of recipes that are centuries old. Even in medieval England—cake came from their word for "flat." These cakes were usually combinations of nuts and honey called *satura*, which was a flat heavy cake.

Baking utensils and directions have been so perfected down through the ages and simplified that today even the amateur cook can become almost an expert. The most revolutionary event in baking through the ages came about during the middle of the 18th century when yeast had fallen into disuse as a raising agent for cakes in favor of beaten eggs. Once as much air as possible had been beaten in, the mixture would be poured into molds, often very elaborate creations, but sometimes as simple as two tin hoops, set on parchment paper on a cookie sheet. It is from these cake hoops that our modern cake pans developed.

By the early nineteenth century, due to the Industrial Revolution, baking ingredients became more affordable and readily available because of mass production and the railroads. Modern leavening agents, such as baking soda and baking powder were invented. (On a day when you're looking for an interesting subject for research, look up the history of baking powder. It is most interesting and it helps to explain why this seemingly insignificant white powder causes certain cake failures.)

I invite you back into my mother's kitchen of the 1930s. It was a time when the success of baking a cake was considered an accomplishment filled with pride by most women—especially when there was an occasion when a cake was carefully taken to the host house of a friend or relative. If a rural homemaker's cake was just a little higher or fluffier—well—that was a source of satisfaction that did much for the homemaker's feeling of self worth. I have within me that same "sense of accomplishment" when a baking venture turns out to be a "pretty sensational presentation."

Again, the recipes included in this chapter on cakes are from my collection of 60+ years of cooking, beginning with some of my mother's. Let us begin—enjoy!

Grandpa Jerry's birthday (1994) celebrating with grandsons Dakota and Jesse Durden.

Mom's Checkerboard Cake

We baked this cake only when we felt adventurous and did not care too much about our presentation. It was just fun and never failed to impress us.

2 cups sugar
1 cup butter
1 cup sweet milk
2 teaspoon baking powder
2 teaspoon vanilla
3 cups flour
6 egg whites, beaten stiff

Divide batter into two parts and color one part with chocolate or cocoa. Have 3 pans greased and floured. Into the first pan put a spoonful of the white batter into center of pan; then a ring of dark around that; then a ring of white around that, and etc. Next, into the center of the second pan put opposite color in center of the first pan and etc. Bake at 350 degrees. and when cool and ready to assemble, put layer with the dark center in the middle layer. Ice with chocolate or white frosting.

Fresh Apple Cake

This recipe came from Charlie Dagher who was the Comfort High School band director in the 1960s. Through Bernice Schaetter we became good friends and his recipe became one of my favorite cakes to bake. More moist than most other apple cake recipes.

4 medium apples (to equal
    4 cups peeled, diced,
    fresh apples)
1 cup pecans, cut up
2 cups white sugar
3 cups flour
1/2 teaspoon nutmeg
1/2 teaspoon cinnamon
1/2 teaspoon salt
2 teaspoons baking soda
1 cup Wesson oil
1 teaspoon vanilla
2 beaten eggs

Mix together apples, pecans, and sugar. Let stand at least 1 hour or longer. Stir often.

Sift together flour, nutmeg, cinnamon, salt, and soda.

Add flour mixture to apple mixture and add oil, vanilla, and eggs. Mix by hand. In large tube pan prepared with oil and flour, bake at 350 degrees for 1 hour 15 minutes.

Chiffon Cake

When we finally bought Mom an electric Sunbeam Mixmaster for Christmas around 1950, this cake became the one that everybody in our world was baking. It was a totally revolutionary cake and created a competition among friends to see who could make the cake rise the highest. Read the "fold in. . . " carefully!

2 cups cake flour
1 1/2 sugar, divided use
1 1/2 teaspoon baking powder
3/4 teaspoon salt
7 eggs, separated plus
  2 egg whites

1/2 cup vegetable oil
3/4 cup milk
1 teaspoon vanilla extract
3/4 teaspoon cream of tartar

Preheat oven to 325 degrees. In a *large* bowl, sift together the cake flour, 1 1/4 cups sugar, baking powder, and salt. Whisk the dry ingredients well to make sure they are thoroughly combined. Make a well in the center of the dry ingredients. Set aside.

Carefully separate 7 eggs—keep whites clear of any yolk.

In a second small bowl, beat the 7 egg yolks. Pour the yolks into the well in the dry ingredients, along with the vegetable oil, milk, and vanilla. Beat the wet ingredients into the dry until completely smooth. Set aside.

In the largest bowl of the stand mixer, beat the 7 egg whites plus 2 more egg whites and cream of tartar until foamy. With the mixer running slowly, rain in the remaining one-fourth cup of sugar. Continue to beat the whites until stiff peaks stay formed when the beater are lifted.

Next, fold the beaten whites into the rest of the batter by gently spooning 1/3 of the beaten egg whites into the large bowl with the batter. Slowly and carefully fold the whites into the batter using a spatula or a whisk until mixed. Add another 1/3 of the beaten whites to the bowl and gently fold into the batter. Be very gentle as you fold in the whites as you do not want to deflate them. *It is the whites that lighten the batter and are largely responsible for the cake's ability to rise as it bakes.* Gently fold in the remaining 1/3 of the whites.

Spoon or gently pour the batter into a 10-inch *ungreased* angel food cake pan. Place the pan in the oven and bake 1 hour to 1 hour

10 minutes or until the cake is puffed (it should rise over the top of the pan by 2 to 3 inches but will deflate a little as it cools. The cake should be lightly browned on top and toothpick or cake tester comes out clean.

Remove from heat and invert the pan over a wine bottle. *Set the pan aside until cooled completely, 1 to 2 hours.* Loosen the sides with a thin knife and tap it gently to remove the cake.

Seven Minute Icing

1 cup Marshmallow fluff
2 egg whites, at room
temperature
1 cup sugar

$^1/_4$ teaspoon cream of tartar
$^1/_8$ teaspoon salt
$^1/_4$ cup water
1 teaspoon vanilla

In double-boiler top—over hot boiling water—combine all above ingredients except vanilla. With hand mixer, beat until soft peaks form. Make sure they are definitely soft and not too stiff at this point. If you get it too thick, it will not spread correctly. Remove from heat and continue beating until stiff. Beat in vanilla. This is really great when dusted with coconut on top.

Layered Banana Crunch Cake

CRUNCH:
1 cup chopped pecans
1 cup coconut
1 cup packed brown sugar

1 cup uncooked oats
$^1/_2$ cup melted butter

Mix all ingredients and set aside.

CAKE:
1 cup sour cream
4 eggs

2 bananas
1 box yellow cake mix

Preheat oven to 350 degrees. Beat together sour cream, eggs, and bananas. Add yellow cake mix and beat for 2 minutes. Alternate layers of cake batter and crunch mix in greased and floured 10-inch tube pan ending with batter on top. Bake until done, about 1 hour.

Oatmeal Cake

1 cup quick-cook oatmeal	2 cups flour
1 teaspoon soda	$^1/_2$ teaspoon cinnamon
1$^1/_2$ cups hot water	1 stick butter
2 cups brown sugar, divided use	1 cup brown sugar
1 cup white sugar	$^1/_2$ cup evaporated milk
$^1/_2$ stick butter	1 teaspoon vanilla
2 eggs	$^1/_2$ cup pecans
$^1/_2$ cup Wesson or Mazola	$^1/_2$ cup coconut

Mix together oatmeal, soda, and hot water. Set aside.

Cream together 1 cup brown sugar, white sugar, butter, eggs, oil, flour, and cinnamon.

Add oatmeal to creamed mixture. Beat only until blended. Bake in well-greased and floured shallow pan at 375 degrees. Bake for about 20 minutes or slightly more. While that is baking, mix together butter, 1 cup brown sugar, evaporated milk, vanilla, pecans, and coconut. At end of baking time, spread this mixture on cake and return to oven for 15 minutes longer.

Pink Cake

This is an oozy, gooey, goodness cake.

1 box white cake mix	$^1/_2$ cup salad oil
1 box strawberry Jell-O	4 eggs
3 tablespoons flour	$^1/_2$ cup frozen strawberries,
$^1/_2$ cup water	thawed, and undrained

To the white cake mix, Jell-O, and flour, add the water and the salad oil and mix thoroughly. Add the eggs one at a time, beating well after each addition. Stir in the thawed strawberries and pour into 2 greased and floured cake pans. Bake at 325 degrees for 25-30 minutes. Cool.

For frosting, cream together $^1/_2$ cup butter, 1 box confectioner's sugar and $^1/_2$ cup undrained strawberries.

> "Vegetables are a must on a diet.
> I suggest carrot cake, zucchini bread, and pumpkin pie."
> —JIM DAVIS, *Garfield*

Texas Jam Cake

1 cup butter, softened	2 teaspoons allspice
1 cup sugar	2 teaspoons cinnamon
5 eggs	¹/₂ teaspoons cloves
1 jar (16-oz.) red plum jam	1 cup buttermilk
1 cup strawberry preserves	maple frosting
3 cups flour	chopped pecans, optional
2 tablespoon soda	

Preheat oven to 350 degrees. In a large mixer bowl, beat butter and sugar until fluffy. Add eggs, one at a time beating well after each addition. Stir in jam and preserves. Stir together dry ingredients and add alternately with buttermilk to jam mixture. Turn into three well-greased, wax paper lined 9" layer cake pans. Bake 40 minutes or until wooden pick inserted near center comes out clean. Cool 5 minutes, remove from pans. Cool completely. Frost with maple frosting and garnish with pecans if desired.

Maple Frosting

In mixer bowl, beat 1 pkg. (8-oz) cream cheese until fluffy. Add 1¹/₂ pounds sifted confectioner's sugar (about 6 cups), 1 or 2 teaspoons maple flavoring and 1 tablespoon milk. Mix well. Add additional milk, 1 teaspoon at a time for desired consistency.

Bill Nelson's granddaughters, Emma and Ali Whitworth, daughters of Martha and Randy of San Antonio, celebrate Emma's birthday. Aunt Sarah Crawford of Houston is helping.

Dirt Cake

This recipe was brought to elementary school's library during a project to collect each child's favorite dessert recipe. This one came from Brodi Reynolds, son of our PE teacher. Brodi went one step further and brought a batch of it to school to prove to us how delicious and fun it was. Follow his directions exactly and take it to your next "pot luck" dinner for dessert. Fun!

1 pkg. (20 oz.) Oreo cookies
1 pkg. (8-oz.) cream cheese
1 cup powdered sugar
1/2 stick butter

2 pkgs. (3.5 oz.) vanilla
   instant pudding
3 1/2 cups milk
1 carton (12 oz.) Cool Whip

Grind Oreos in food processor until they look like potting soil. Set aside.

Cream together cream cheese, sugar, and butter, and set aside.

Blend together the 2 packages pudding and milk. Combine with cream cheese mixture and mix.

Use a *new* hanging basket and alternately layer Cool Whip, Oreo cookies, and the pudding mixture. Layer this about three times. *Be sure to end with cookies on top.* Cover and chill overnight. Before taking to the event, decorate with artificial flower in middle of hanging basket and place gummy worms just coming up out of the dirt. Serve with small shovel or digger. Your guests will not soon forget you!

The newest member of the Durden clan is Luke Anthony Durden, son of Roger and Pam, shown with his first birthday chocolate cake.

Chocolate Cake

Carol Giles gave this recipe to all women bringing cakes to our fund raiser. It is very easy and good. Try it—surpasses most chocolate cakes.

2 cups flour	1 cup water
2 cups sugar	$^1/_2$ cup vegetable oil
1 tablespoon baking soda	$^1/_2$ cup buttermilk
1 stick butter	2 eggs
3 tablespoons plus	1 teaspoon vanilla
1$^1/_2$ teaspoons cocoa	

Place flour, sugar, and baking soda in bowl, mix, and set aside. In a saucepan, mix butter, cocoa, water, and oil and bring just to boiling point. Pour over flour and sugar mixture. Mix and add buttermilk, eggs, and vanilla. Mix well.

Pour into 9"×13" pan. Bake for 45-50 minutes until cake is done. Test with toothpick for doneness. Frost while warm.

Chocolate Frosting

1 stick butter	4 cups powdered sugar
3 tablespoons plus	1 cup coarsely chopped pecans
1$^1/_2$ teaspoons cocoa	1 teaspoon vanilla
3 tablespoons milk	

Bring just to boiling butter, cocoa, and milk. In bowl, mix powdered sugar, pecans, and vanilla. Pour butter mixture into sugar mixture and mix until smooth. Spread on warm cake.

"Who discovered we could get milk from cows, and what did he think he was doing at the time?"
—BILLY CONNOLLY, comedian

"Best-Ever" Chocolate Cake

$^3/_4$ cup butter	$^3/_4$ teaspoon baking powder
3 eggs	$^1/_2$ teaspoon salt
2 cup flour	2 cups sugar
$^3/_4$ cup unsweetened	1 teaspoon vanilla
cocoa powder	$1^1/_2$ cup milk
1 tsp. baking soda	

Allow butter and eggs to stand at room temperature for 30 minutes. Lightly grease bottom of three 8"×1$^1/_2$" round cake pans. Line bottoms of pans with waxed paper. Grease and lightly flour waxed paper and sides of pans. Set aside.

Preheat oven to 350 degrees. In a medium bowl, stir together flour, cocoa powder, baking soda, baking powder, and salt. Set aside.

In a large mixing bowl beat butter with an electric mixer on medium to high speed for 30 seconds. Gradually add sugar about $^1/_4$ cup at a time, beating on medium speed for 3-4 minutes or until well mixed. Scrape sides of bowl, continue beating on medium speed for 2 minutes. Add eggs, one at a time, beating after each addition (about 1 minute total). Beat in vanilla. Alternately add flour mixture and milk to beaten mixture, beating on low speed just until combined after each addition. Beat on medium to high speed for 20 seconds more. Spread evenly into prepared pans.

Bake for 30-35 minutes or until wooden pick comes out clean. Cool cake layers in pans for 10 minutes. Remove from pans. Peel waxed paper. Cool completely on wire racks.

Prepare chocolate frosting and frost cake layers.

Chocolate Frosting

1 pkg. (12-oz. or 2 cups)	1 carton (8-oz.) dairy sour cream
semi-sweet chocolate pieces	$4^1/_2$ cups sifted powdered sugar
$^1/_2$ cup butter	

In a large saucepan, combine semisweet chocolate pieces and butter. Heat over low heat until melted, stirring often. Cool for 5 minutes. Stir in sour cream. Gradually add powdered sugar, beating on medium speed until mixture is smooth.

Hot Fudge Pudding Cake

1 ¼ cups sugar, divided use
1 cup flour
½ cup cocoa powder,
  divided use
2 teaspoons baking powder
¼ teaspoon salt
½ cup milk

⅓ cup butter, melted
1 ½ teaspoon vanilla
½ cup packed light
  brown sugar
1 ¼ cups hot water
Cool Whip

Heat oven to 350 degrees. Combine ¾ cup sugar, flour, ¼ cup cocoa, baking powder, and salt. Stir in milk, butter, and vanilla and beat until smooth. Pour batter into ungreased 9" square baking pan.

Stir together remaining ½ cup sugar, brown sugar, and remaining ¼ cup cocoa. Sprinkle mixture evenly over batter. Pour hot water over top. *Do not stir.*

Bake 35-40 minutes or until center is almost set. Remove from oven and let stand for 15 minutes. Serve in dessert dishes, spooning sauce from pan over top. Garnish with Cool Whip if desired. 8 servings.

Always around the table, inspired by good food, the family tends to become nostalgic about "those growing up years." From left to right: Don Durden, James Durden, Roger Durden, Pam Norini Durden, Monica Wallace, the author, Mae Durden-Nelson, and Susan Rose Durden.

Carrot cake was another one of those phenomenal recipes that hit the kitchens of America and took cake bakers everywhere by storm. It was not long before many variations followed. Since most everyone  *has their favorite carrot layer cake, I am including two different recipes baked in a 9"×13" pan that are certain winners and much easier than the original cake.*

Game Dinner Carrot Cake

2 cups sugar
1 1/2 cups vegetable oil
3 eggs
2 cups flour
1 teaspoon baking soda
2 teaspoons cinnamon
1 teaspoon salt

2 cups grated carrots
1 cup chopped nuts
1 cup coconut
1 (8-oz.) can crushed
   pineapple (drained)
1 teaspoon vanilla

Beat together sugar, oil, and eggs. Add flour, baking soda, cinnamon, and salt. Mix well, then fold in carrots, nuts, coconut, pineapple, and vanilla. Bake at 325 degrees about 1 hour. Test for doneness. Cool and frost. Makes 15 generous servings.

Carrot Cake Frosting

4 oz. softened cream cheese
1 teaspoon vanilla

2 cups powdered sugar
1/4 cup butter

Mix ingredients until smooth and spread over cake.

Lillian Hahn's Carrot Cake
extra moist

2 cups sugar
1 cup salad oil
2 eggs
3 cups flour
1 crushed pineapple
   (8.5 oz.) with juice
1 cup pecans

1 cup raisins
2 teaspoons baking soda
1/2 teaspoon salt
1/2 teaspoon salt
2 teaspoons cinnamon
3 cups grated carrots

Mix sugar and salad oil. Add eggs and beat well. Gradually add all other ingredients—stirring by hand. Bake in 9"×13" pan for 1 hour at 325 degrees. Make topping by bringing to a boil and pour over hot cake: 1 cup sugar, 1/2 cup orange juice, and 1 teaspoon orange rind. Freezes well.

Beet Pound Cake with Orange Glaze

I baked this cake for a second Sunday lunch at our St. Boniface Episcopal Church simply because it was so different. Several people kept going back for seconds commenting that it was "so good!" Finally, came the question, "Who baked this cake?" I confessed. The most heard reply was, "This is an awesome cake and I don't even like beets!"

1 jar (16 oz.) sliced pickled
   beets, drained
2¼ cups sugar, divided use
1¼ cups dried sweetened
   cranberries
2½ cups flour
1½ teaspoons baking powder
1 teaspoons baking soda
½ teaspoon salt
1 teaspoon cinnamon

½ teaspoon nutmeg
4 large eggs, room temperature
1½ sticks unsalted butter,
   very soft
¼ cup vegetable oil
Finely grated zest from 1 orange
2 teaspoons vanilla extract
½ cup buttermilk
Orange Glaze (recipe on top
   of next page)

Preheat oven to 350 degrees. Butter and flour 10" Bundt pan.

Place drained beets and 1 cup sugar in food processor. Process to a smooth puree, scraping down sides of bowl once. Place cranberries in small bowl, adding enough hot water to cover. Sift together flour, baking powder, baking soda, salt, cinnamon, and nutmeg. Set aside.

Combine remaining 1¼ cups sugar, eggs, butter, and vegetable oil in large mixing bowl. With electric mixer, beat on medium high 2-3 minutes until light and smooth. Blend in beet puree. Stir in orange zest and vanilla.

Add half of flour mixture to beet mixture and beat on low speed until smooth. Add buttermilk; beat on slow speed until smooth. Add the remaining flour mixture, beating until uniform.

Drain cranberries well; fold into batter. Spoon batter into prepared pan, spreading evenly. Bake on center oven rack about 45-50 minutes, until cake pulls away from the sides of pan and toothpick inserted into center of cake comes out clean.

Place pan on cooling rack for 15 minutes, then invert cake onto cooling rack. Cool briefly.

Orange Glaze

2¹/₂ cups confectioner's sugar   ¹/₄ cup orange juice
grated zest of 1 orange   1¹/₂ tablespoons butter, melted

In large bowl, combine confectioner's sugar and zest. Add orange juice and whisk until smooth. Whisk in butter, adding additional juice if necessary for consistency. Spoon over warm cake and sprinkle with pecans if desired.

Fruit Cocktail Cake
Unique cake from South Dakota via Judy Ablin

2 eggs   2 cups flour
1¹/₂ cups sugar   1¹/₂ teaspoons baking soda
1 can (#303) fruit cocktail   ¹/₂ cup coconut
  with juice   ¹/₂ cup brown sugar
1 teaspoon vanilla

Beat eggs until foaming and thick. Add sugar and beat well. Add fruit cocktail with juice and vanilla. Mix in flour and baking soda. Put in 9"×13" pan and sprinkle with coconut and brown sugar. Bake 1 hour at 275 degrees. Slightly cool cake when done and pour Easy Icing over top. Serve warm.

Easy Icing

1 stick butter   1 small can evaporated
³/₄ cup sugar   milk (3/4 cup)
¹/₂ cup pecans

Mix butter, sugar, and milk in saucepan. Boil 2 minutes and add pecans.

"Some people like to paint pictures, or do gardening, or build a boat in the basement. Other people get a tremendous pleasure out of the kitchen, because cooking is just as creative and imaginative an activity as drawing, or wood carving, or music."

—JULIA CHILD

Pineapple Upside-Down Surprise Cake

1 can (8-oz.) crushed pineapple	3 1/3 cups cake flour,
4 tablespoons, plus	minus 2 tablespoons
2/3 cup butter (divided use)	5 teaspoons baking powder
8 oz. Habanera Hula Jam	1/2 teaspoon salt
(Pineapple-Habanera jam)	1 1/2 cups sugar
1 cup brown sugar, firmly packed	2 eggs
1 can (4-oz.) pineapple rings	1 tablespoon vanilla

Preheat oven to 350 degrees. Drain crushed pineapple, reserving the pineapple and the juice separately. Add enough water to the juice to make a total of 1 1/3 cups liquid. Set aside.

Put 4 tablespoons butter in a 9"×13" baking pan and set it into the oven to melt the butter. Mix together the drained crushed pineapple and pineapple-habanera jam. Remove the pan from oven and mix the brown sugar with the melted butter into the pan. Add the pineapple mixture spreading it evenly across the bottom of the pan. Place the pineapple rings in an even layer on top of this mixture. Set aside.

Combine flour, baking powder, and salt in a bowl. In a larger bowl, beat the remaining 2/3 cup of butter for 30 seconds with mixer. Add the white sugar and beat until well combined. Add eggs and vanilla, beating for 1 minute more. Add dry ingredients and pineapple liquid alternately, in batches, to the butter mixture, mixing until all ingredients are combined.

Spread the batter evenly over the pineapples in the baking pan. Bake for 30-35 minutes or until toothpick in center comes out clean. Remove the pan from the oven and immediately invert it onto a serving platter. Let cake cool before serving. Makes 16 servings.

Pineapple Right-Side-Up Cake

2 eggs
1$^1/_2$ cups sugar
1 teaspoon vanilla
1 can (20-oz.) crushed
   pineapple, divided use

2$^1/_4$ cups flour
1$^1/_2$ teaspoons baking soda
$^1/_2$ teaspoon salt
$^1/_2$ cup chopped pecans

Preheat oven to 350 degrees. Beat eggs with electric mixer. Gradually add sugar and vanilla. Continue beating mixture until it is a lemon color. Change speed to low and alternately add half the pineapple (undrained) and dry ingredients. Spread batter on a lightly greased 15"×10" inch jelly roll pan. Sprinkle pecans over top. Bake for 19-20 minutes or until top is golden brown. Pour remaining pineapple (slightly drained) over cake.

Right-Side-Up Glaze

$^1/_3$ cup evaporated milk
$^3/_4$ cups confectioner's sugar

$^1/_2$ cup butter

Boil all ingredients 3-4 minutes until white and bubbly. Pour glaze over top while cake is still warm. Refrigerate for a few hours before serving. Serves 10 to 12.

Heavenly Cake

1 box white cake mix
1 can (3.5 oz.) sweetened
   flaked coconut
1 cup chopped nuts

$^1/_4$ cup butter
8 oz. cream cheese, softened
1 box (6 oz.) powdered sugar

Preheat oven to 350 degrees. Grease a 9"×13" baking pan. Prepare cake batter according to package instructions. Cover the bottom of the pan with nuts and coconut. Pour cake batter evenly over the bottom.

Melt butter in a medium size pan and add the cream cheese and sugar. Mix well and spoon cream cheese mixture over the batter. Bake for 40-42 minutes. You can't test this cake for doneness because it is so gooey.

Calvin's German Chocolate Cake

1 box German chocolate
  cake mix
1 jar (12-oz.) caramel topping
1 can sweetened condensed milk

1 pkg. (8-oz.) Cool Whip
Heath toffee bits or Heath bars,
  chopped

Preheat oven to 350 degrees. Prepare cake mix according to package instructions. Bake in a 9"×13" pan until done. While still hot, poke holes in the cake with the handle of a wooden spoon. Mix together caramel sauce and sweetened condensed milk. Pour evenly over cake. Allow cake to cool. Serve with generous dollop of whipped topping evenly over top of cake serving and sprinkle generously with toffee bits and cherry on top. *Sinful!*

Quick Unique Cake
More from Judy Ablin, South Dakota

1 cup sugar
1 cup butter
2 egg yolks

1 teaspoon vanilla
1 cup flour
1 teaspoon baking powder

Cream butter and sugar. Add egg yolks and vanilla and beat well. Sift flour and baking powder twice and add to creamed mixture. Turn into 9"×13" pan and top with the following: Into the two beaten egg whites, fold in 1 1/2 cups brown sugar, 1 1/2 cups pecans, and 1/2 teaspoon vanilla. Spread on cake batter and bake 20 minutes at 325 degrees.

Celebrating her birthday is Kristin Durden, Daughter of James Durden. Kristin is the first Durden female to be born in sixty years.

Neiman Marcus German Cake
extravagant rich flavor

1 box German chocolate cake mix	2 eggs
	¹/₂ cup chopped pecans
¹/₂ cup butter, melted and cooled	

Preheat oven to 350 degrees. Mix cake mix with butter, eggs, and pecans. Grease 9"×13" pan and pat mixture into pan. Set aside.

Unbaked Cake Topping

1 pkg. (8-oz.) cream cheese	1 teaspoon vanilla
1 box (16-oz.) powdered sugar	¹/₂ cup chopped pecans
2 eggs, beaten	

Combine ingredients and spread over unbaked cake mixture. Bake 30 minutes, cool, and serve.

German Chocolate Upside-Down Cake

1 cup flaked coconut	1¹/₄ cup water
1 cup chopped pecans	¹/₄ cup vegetable oil
1 pkg. (18-24 oz.) German chocolate cake mix	1 pkg. (8-oz.) cream cheese
	¹/₂ cup butter
3 large eggs	1 pound powdered sugar, sifted

Grease a 13"×9"×2" inch pan. Line with wax paper and grease the paper. Sprinkle coconut and pecans in the bottom of prepared pan. Set aside.

Combine cake mix, eggs, water, and oil in a large bowl and mix according to package directions. Spoon batter over coconut and pecans.

Combine cream cheese and butter in a saucepan and cook over low heat, stirring often until butter melts and mixture is smooth. Stir in powdered sugar. Spoon mixture evenly over batter.

Bake at 350 degrees for 40-45 minutes. Cool in pan on a wire rack for 10 minutes. Invert cake onto a serving plate and remove wax paper and discard.

German Chocolate Carrot Cake

3 cups flour
2 cups sugar
2 (1-oz.) squares German
  sweet chocolate, grated
2 teaspoon cinnamon
1 1/2 teaspoons baking soda
1 1/2 teaspoons salt
1 teaspoon baking powder

1 (8-oz.) can crushed
  pineapple, drained
3 large eggs
1 1/2 cups vegetable oil
2 teaspoons vanilla
2 cups peeled, grated
  raw carrots
1 1/2 cups finely chopped pecans

Heat oven to 350 degrees. Grease and dust with flour a 10-12 cup Bundt pan. In bowl of electric mixer, combine flour, sugar, chocolate, cinnamon, baking soda, salt, and baking powder. Mix on low to blend. Add pineapple, eggs, vegetable oil, and vanilla. Beat on medium speed 3-4 minutes. By hand, fold in carrots and pecans. Pour into prepared pan. Bake about 75-90 minutes or until tester comes out clean. Cool in pan 10 minutes.

Remove cake from pan and place on rack. Cool completely. Frost with cream cheese frosting.

Cream Cheese Frosting

2 1/2 cups powdered sugar
1/2 pkg. (8-oz.) cream cheese,
  room temperature
3 tablespoons butter,
  room temperature

1 tablespoon vanilla
1-2 tablespoons milk
1/4 cup chopped pecans
1/4 cup raisins

In bowl of electric mixer, combine powdered sugar, cream cheese, butter, vanilla, and milk. Mix on medium speed until smooth and creamy. By hand, stir in pecans and raisins.

Is it the cake or the frosting that is your favorite? Or both together! Yummy!

Coca-Cola Cake

1 cup Coca-Cola	2 large eggs, lightly beaten
½ cup buttermilk	2 teaspoons vanilla
2 cups flour	1½ cups miniature
¼ cup cocoa	marshmallows
1 teaspoon baking soda	¾ cup pecans, chopped
1 cup butter, softened	and toasted
1¾ cups sugar	Coca-Cola frosting (follows)

Preheat oven to 350 degrees. Grease and flour a 9"×13" pan.

Combine Coca-Cola and buttermilk; set side. Combine flour, cocoa, and baking soda; set aside.

In a medium mixing bowl beat butter at low speed with electric mixer until creamy. Gradually add sugar; beat until blended. Add eggs and vanilla; beat at low speed until blended. Add cocoa-flour mixture alternately with cola mixture; begin and end with dry ingredients. Beat at low speed just until blended. Stir in marshmallows. Pour batter into prepared pan. Bake for 30-35 minutes. Remove from oven allow to cool for 10 minutes. Pour Coca-Cola Frosting over warm cake; top off with toasted pecans. Serves 20.

Coca-Cola Frosting

½ cup butter	1 pkg. (16 oz.) confectioner's
⅓ cup Coca Cola	sugar
3 tablespoons cocoa	1 tablespoon vanilla

In a large saucepan over medium heat bring butter, Coca-Cola, and cocoa to a boil, stirring until butter melts. Remove from heat and whisk in confectioner's sugar and vanilla.

On May 8, 1886, Coca Cola was invented by Dr. John Pemberton, a pharmacist from Atlanta, Georgia. John Pemberton concocted the Coca Cola formula in a three legged brass kettle in his backyard. The name was a suggestion given by John Pemberton's bookkeeper Frank Robinson, who also had excellent penmanship. It was he who first scripted "Coca Cola" into the flowing letters which has become the famous logo of today.

Whipping Cream Pound Cake

3 cups sugar
3 sticks butter (softened)
6 eggs

3 cups sifted cake flour
$1/2$ pint heavy whipping cream
$1/2$ teaspoon vanilla

Do not preheat oven.

In a large bowl, combine sugar and butter until creamy. Add eggs one at a time. When well mixed add flour and whipping cream alternately. Then add vanilla. Pour into well greased tube pan. Bake at 300 degrees for $1^{1}/_{2}$ hours. Cool completely.

Pound Cake Glaze

2 cups sifted powdered sugar
$1/4$ cup butter, melted
2-4 tablespoons heavy cream

$1/4$ vanilla or almond flavoring,
if desired

Combine powdered sugar and butter in a medium bowl. Stir in 2 tablespoons heavy cream and vanilla or almond. Beat until smooth and creamy. Add more cream if necessary. Drizzle over cool cake.

Fool You Angel Food Cake

1 box low-fat angel
 food cake mix
1 can no-sugar pie cherries

1 teaspoon vanilla
1 teaspoon almond extract

Mix cake mix, pie cherries, vanilla, and almond extract. Bake in 9"×13" pan at 350 degrees for 40 minutes. Enjoy!

"From morning till night, sounds drift from the kitchen, most of them familiar and comforting. On days when warmth is the most important need of the human heart, the kitchen is the place you can find it; it dries the wet sock, it cools the hot little brain."
—E. B. WHITE (1899-1985)

Esther's Orange Marmalade Layer Cake

This recipe was finally revealed on the Internet in response to wide public requests from the multitude of readers of the Mitford Series written by Jan Karon during the early 1990s.
This cake takes a lot of time and work but the final presentation is truly awesome!

CAKE:

3 cups cake flour
1/2 teaspoon baking soda
1/2 teaspoon salt
1 cup softened unsalted butter
2 cups sugar
3 large eggs, at room
   temperature, beaten lightly

1 tablespoon grated orange zest
1 1/2 teaspoons vanilla
1 cup buttermilk,
   at room temperature

Preheat oven to 325 degrees. Butter two 9" round cake pans, line with parchment or waxed paper. Butter and flour the paper, shaking out the excess.

In a bowl, sift the flour, baking soda, and salt.

In a bowl with an electric mixer, beat the butter until combined, add the sugar, a little at a time, and beat the mixture until light and fluffy. Beat in the eggs, orange zest, and vanilla. Beat in 1/3 of the dry ingredients alternately with 1/2 of the buttermilk until combined well. Add half the remaining dry ingredients and the remaining buttermilk and beat until combined well. Finally, beat in the remaining dry ingredients until mixture is smooth.

Evenly divide the batter between the pans, smooth the surface, rap each pan on the counter to expel any air pockets or bubbles. Then transfer to the oven. Bake for 45 minutes or until cake tester comes out clean. Transfer to racks and cool in the pans for 20 minutes.

ORANGE SYRUP:

1 cup freshly squeezed
   orange juice

1/4 cup sugar

In a bowl, stir together orange juice and sugar until sugar is dissolved.

(continued on next page)

FILLING:
1 cup orange marmalade
In a small saucepan set over moderate heat, heat the marmalade until just melted. Let cool 5 minutes.

FROSTING:
³/₄ cup well-chilled heavy cream   ³/₄ cup well-chilled sour cream
3 tablespoons sugar

In a bowl, whisk the heavy cream with the sugar until it forms firm peaks. Add sour cream, a little at a time, and whisk to spreading consistency.

ASSEMBLE THE CAKE:
Arrange one of the layers on a cake plate and carefully peel off the waxed paper, then spread ²/₃ of the marmalade over the top, smoothing it into an even layer. Invert the remaining layer onto the top of the first layer, peel off waxed paper, and spoon the remaining marmalade onto the center of it, leaving a 1¹/₄-inch border around the edge. Frost the sides and top border with the frosting, leaving the marmalade on top of the cake exposed. Chill for at least 2 hours before serving—better overnight.

Earthquake Cake

1 box German chocolate   1 cup pecans, chopped
  cake mix   ¹/₄ cup butter
1 can (3.5 oz.) sweetened   8-oz. cream cheese, softened
  flaked coconut   1 box (16 oz.) powdered sugar

Preheat oven to 350 degrees. Prepare cake batter according to directions. Grease a 9"×13" baking pan and cover the bottom with nuts and coconut. Pour cake batter on top.
Melt butter in a bowl and add cream cheese and powdered sugar. Stir to blend. Spoon over unbaked batter and bake for 40 to 45 minutes. You can't test for doneness as it is a sticky cake. The icing sinks to the bottom while baking and makes a gooey white ribbon throughout the cake. To serve this dessert, use a bowl and add chocolate chips, whipped cream, and cherry on top.

Better Than Sex Cake

CAKE:

1 box Duncan Hines butter
   cake mix
1 (8-oz.) package chocolate
   chips
1 (8-oz.) pecans, chopped
1 (4 serving size) box instant
   vanilla pudding mix
1/2 package unsweetened German
   chocolate bar, grated

1 (8-oz.) carton dairy sour cream
1/2 cup vegetable oil
1/2 cup milk
4 eggs
1 stick unsalted butter,
   at room temperature

Preheat the oven to 350 degrees. Mix all cake ingredients. Pour into a greased and floured Bundt pan. Bake 1 hour. When the cake is cool, make the icing.

Cream Cheese and Coconut Icing

1 (8-oz.) cream cheese,
   at room temperature
1 (16-oz.) box powdered sugar

1 teaspoon vanilla
Chopped nuts
Flaked coconut

Cream together the cream cheese and sugar. Add vanilla. Ice the cake, then sprinkle cake with the nuts and coconut.

Slap Me Naked Cake
Recipe from Robin Hale

1 box German chocolate
   cake mix
1 can sweetened
   condensed milk
4 Heath candy bars

1 jar caramel sauce
Chocolate sauce
Cool Whip
3 candy bars of your choice

Bake cake as directed in 9"×13" pan. While cake is still warm, poke holes in the cake with the handle of a wooden spoon. Pour can of condensed milk over the cake and sprinkle with crushed Heath or Skor bars. Drizzle with caramel sauce and chocolate sauce. Chill. Cover with Cool Whip then with 3 more crushed candy bars. Drizzle with caramel and chocolate sauce. Wow!

CHAPTER FIVE

Favorite Specialty Desserts

Peach Sundae with Cayenne Bourbon Sauce

1 tablespoon lemon juice
2 large ripe peaches, peeled,
   pitted, thinly sliced
6 tablespoons unsalted butter
$\frac{1}{2}$ cup firmly packed
   light brown sugar

$\frac{1}{2}$ teaspoon cayenne powder
3 tablespoons whipping cream
$\frac{1}{2}$ cup chopped pecan
   pieces, toasted
1 tablespoon bourbon
1 pint vanilla ice cream

Combine lemon juice and peach slices in a medium bowl, tossing the peaches to coat them with the juice. Set aside.

Melt the butter in a heavy, medium-sized saucepan over medium heat. Add brown sugar and cayenne, and stir until the mixture thickens and bubbles. Add the whipping cream, 1 tablespoon at a time, stirring until the sugar has dissolved and the sauce is thick and smooth (about 3 minutes).

Stir in the peach mixture, pecans, and bourbon. Cook 1 minute longer, stirring constantly, until the sauce is heated through. Scoop the ice cream into bowls and spoon the sauce over it. Makes 4 servings.

"No diet will remove all the fat from your body because the brain is entirely fat. Without a brain you might look good, but all you could do is run for public office."

—COVERT BAILEY (fitness expert)

Grape and Apple Crisp

FILLING:

6 cups thinly sliced
  peeled tart apples
2 cups seedless red grapes

$^1/_3$ cup orange juice
$1^1/_2$ tablespoons flour
2 tablespoons sugar

Preheat oven to 375 degrees. Combine all ingredients in a 2-quart baking pan.

TOPPING

$^3/_4$ cup flour
$^3/_4$ cups old-fashioned oats
$^1/_3$ cup chopped pecans
6 tablespoon brown sugar

$^3/_4$ cup ($1^1/_2$ sticks) cold,
  unsalted butter, cut into
  small pieces

Combine flour, oats, pecans, and brown sugar. Add butter and use a pastry cutter to combine until mixture resembles coarse crumbs. Sprinkle over the apples and bake 45 minutes or until golden brown and apples are tender. Cool. Serves 8.

Apple Peanut Butter Crisp

6-8 green apples,
  pared and sliced
$^1/_2$ cup water
2 tablespoons lemon juice
1 tablespoon cinnamon

$^3/_4$ cup flour
$^3/_4$ cup brown sugar
$^1/_3$ cup peanut butter
$^1/_4$ cup butter

Preheat oven to 350 degrees. Arrange apples slices in bottom of a lightly oiled 9"×13" baking dish. Mix water and lemon juice and pour over apples. Sprinkle cinnamon on top. Mix remaining ingredients until crumbly. Spread evenly over the apples and bake for about 40 minutes or until golden brown. Serve with small scoop vanilla ice cream.

BONUS: Mix tablespoon of caramel sauce with a tablespoon of peanut butter as sauce over top!

Dump Cake
(Deserves a Better Name)

1 (20-oz.) can crushed
pineapple in heavy syrup,
undrained
1 (21-oz.) can of cherry
pie filling

1 package yellow cake mix
1 cup pecans, chopped
$^1/_2$ (1 stick) butter

Preheat oven to 350 degrees. Grease 9" × 13" baking pan.

Spread the pineapple with its syrup evenly in pan. Spoon the cherry pie filling evenly over the pineapple. Sprinkle the dry cake mix evenly over the above ingredients. Sprinkle chopped pecans over the cake mix. Cut chilled butter in thin slices and place them evenly on top of the nuts. Bake 50 minutes until golden.

Quick Apple Dumplings

1 pkg. (8-count) refrigerated
crescent roll dough
2 medium Granny Smith
apples, peeled, cored
and quartered
$^1/_8$ teaspoon cinnamon

$^1/_2$ cup butter
1 cup sugar
1 cup orange juice
1 teaspoon vanilla
$^1/_2$ cup very finely
chopped pecans

Preheat oven to 350 degrees. Grease an 8" square baking dish.

Unroll and separate crescent roll dough. Wrap each apple fourth in a crescent roll. Place in pan. Sprinkle with cinnamon.

Combine butter, sugar, and orange juice in a medium saucepan. Bring to a boil. Remove from heat and stir in vanilla. Pour over dumplings. Sprinkle pecans over top.

Bake 30 minutes or until crust is golden and beginning to bubble and apples are tender when pierced with a fork.

Serve, spoon some of the syrup from the baking dish over dumplings. Serve with touch of ice cream. Serves 8.

> "There is one thing more exasperating than a wife who can cook and won't and that's a wife who can't cook and will."
>
> —ROBERT FROST (1847-1963)

Apple Rolls

This recipe goes back to early 1951 when I was just married and a rancher's wife. It comes from Norma (Rode) Geistweidt who made it for our lunch dessert one day when our husbands joined forces for a long forgotten ranch project.

2 cups flour
4 teaspoons baking powder
$^1/_2$ teaspoon salt
3 tablespoons shortening

$^1/_2$ cup liquid ($^1/_4$ cup water plus $^1/_4$ cup milk)
4 apples, chopped fine

Mix first 5 ingredients together for dough. Roll out $^1/_2$-inch thick and spread with chopped apples. Roll up like jelly roll and cut into $1^1/_2$ or 2-inch long pieces. Place cut side down in hot syrup made by boiling 1 pint water and $1^1/_2$ cups sugar. Put pieces of butter on top of each roll and sprinkle with sugar and nutmeg. Bake 30 minutes at 350 degrees. Serve warm—ice cream optional.

Butterfinger Dessert

2 cups milk
1 quart vanilla ice cream
2 (3.5 oz.) instant vanilla
   pudding
$^1/_2$ cup butter
$1^1/_2$ crushed graham
   cracker crumbs

$^1/_2$ cup crushed saltine crackers
1 (8-oz.) Cool Whip topping
4 (2-oz) Butterfinger
   candy bars, crushed

Combine milk, ice cream, and dry pudding mix in a large bowl and beat until well mixed. Place in refrigerator.

Melt butter and pour over cracker crumbs in a large bowl. Stir well and pour into a 13"×9" pan, patting into an even layer on bottom and reserving $^1/_3$ of the mixture for topping.

Pour ice cream mixture over crust. Freeze 1 hour. Spread Cool Whip topping over filling.

Mix crushed Butterfingers with reserved crumb mixture and sprinkle over top and return to freezer to set. Garnish with chocolate sauce. Serves 10-12.

Pineapple Chiffon Dessert

The first time I ate this dessert was at a Jr. Literary Society meeting at Jackie Busbee's house in 1962. I shall never forget how it impressed me as being the best most delicious dessert I'd ever eaten. Try it—see if you agree.

1 envelope Knox gelatin	$^1/_4$ teaspoon salt
$^1/_4$ cup cold water	Famous Chocolate Wafers
3 slightly beaten egg yolks	3 egg whites
1 can crushed pineapple	$^1/_3$ cup sugar
with syrup (large size)	$^1/_2$ pint whipping cream
1 tablespoon lemon juice	1 tablespoon lemon juice

Soften gelatin in cold water. Set aside. Combine egg yolks, crushed pineapple, lemon juice, and salt in top of double boiler. Cook over hot water, stirring constantly until custard consistency. Stir in gelatin until dissolved. Cool mixture by setting pot in cold water.

Beat egg whites and sugar until *very stiff*. Fold egg white mixture into the cooled custard. Whip cream and lemon juice. Fold whipped cream into mixture. Spoon $^1/_4$ mixture into a greased loaf pan or jelly roll pan. Place Famous Chocolate Wafers on top of custard. Continue to layer—making top layer custard. Chill overnight and serve with a dollop of whipped cream.

Date Marshmallow Log

This recipe is in The Hahn Family Recipes *that was published by Rhea (Hahn) Hill. It was submitted by Helen Hahn, my sister-in-law)*

45 graham crackers	3 cups pecans, chopped
24 large marshmallows,	1$^1/_2$ cups heavy cream
diced	(not whipped)
1$^1/_2$ cups dates, chopped	

Roll graham crackers to fine crumbs. Combine marshmallows, dates and pecans. Mix with 2$^3/_4$ cups cracker crumbs. Add cream and mix thoroughly. Shape into a roll, about 3$^1/_2$ inches across. Roll in remaining cracker crumbs. Wrap well in waxed paper and chill in refrigerator. Cut in $^3/_4$ inch slices to serve topped with whipped cream.

CHAPTER SIX

Main Courses and Casseroles

Having completely gone through my recipe collection of the sweet kind, I confess they represent only about forty percent of my entire assortment. It is embarrassing that I have such a niggling weakness for sweets. (I suppose there are worse things!)

Anyway, I've now spread out my bundle of main course recipes and I am surprised that I don't have very many. I pondered the why of that and came to the conclusion that I grew up not having much experience with the "casserole." I grew up in the middle of five children and very possibly in the mindset of the depression era, a casserole would not have met the needs of a large family or a hungry crew of workers. We often had to prepare the noon meal for a crew of 8 to 12 men who gathered on our farm and ranch to do such hard physical back-breaking labor as butchering/sausage making, shearing goats and sheep, and/or harvesting crops from the field. As I remember it, we mostly served large roasters full of meat baked in our oven accompanied by side-dishes so numerous that the entire table was overloaded with food.

In the summer, when the need arose for a lot of meat, it came from one of our own sheep or goats that my father slaughtered. Or, it was beef that came from our weekly rural "butcher club." A butcher club membership was comprised of a group of select neighbors in the vicinity of our farm. Each member was responsible to raise and special feed and fatten a calf to supply the club for at least one week during the summer. Each member was assigned a week when he would be responsible to have his calf butchered and cut up into meat sections. Then, the entire divided up beef was brought to

Lange's Mill on that given date at a certain set time. All other members were then responsible to bring a personal container and be there on time to pick up his weekly rotation of meat cuts: i.e., forelegs, hind legs, neck, ribs, etc. By the time summer was over and the last week of butcher club came around, each household will have consumed an entire calf.

It is important to remember that refrigeration, as we know it today, was not yet available to us during the 1930s and early 1940s. Preservation of food, especially meat, was a definite problem during the hot Texas summer months. However, most farm families were large and they had no problem consuming their particular cut of meat in seven days' time. In fact, it was up to the farmer's wife to make sure the meat lasted a week.

Interestingly, I don't remember ever going hungry at any meal in our house, especially with all the other things that were grown in our large garden. Using the term "plentiful" is not a misnomer! I remember how often we had dozens and dozens of tomatoes spread out on newspapers on the back porch. We consumed a lot of them and the rest were canned and saved for the winter months. It was the same with other surplus vegetables like green beans, okra, etc. By the end of summer there were countless quart jars containing fruits and vegetables all standing in neat rows in our cool cellar, in preparation for the winter.

Returning for a moment to the subject of hunger, I do admit that as little children, we did often wonder if anything would be left for us to eat after a large work crew had finished eating. The working men always ate first and the children came last. That was understood and you did not argue about that. We did make it a point to wander into the dining room if the men lingered too long after completing their meal. That happened a lot. These men, generally good friends and neighbors, came together to get a job done and conversation was enjoyed only during the noon meal. And enjoy each other they did. Germans—it seems to me—were always a joyful lot and they loved to laugh and joke when they got together. That statement surely will bring up the question if they drank beer before or with these meals and I have to say absolutely not. The reason for that was that working with farm machinery during that era was dangerous work—one miscue and you could lose a finger, a hand, an arm, and be badly injured. In our case, such an emergency would have been a seventeen-mile trip over a rough dirt road to the nearest town to see a doctor. That being so, consumption of beer just did not happen on a work day. Weekends? How well do you know the German culture?

Reminiscing again on those early days with my Momma cooking for a crew, I recall also that my mother took great pride in planning her meals for a crew of workers. She was always concerned that we should prepare not only a delicious meal but also that there was enough food so that no man should leave her table hungry. Men's work on the farm and ranch was then and is still today very difficult, physically demanding, and backbreaking. Such labor resulted in very large appetites at the noon dinner table. Which reminds me of another interesting ritual that happened just before mealtime. It was our responsibility to prepare a place outdoors under our large grape arbor with a large "wash pan" and a large water container along with a bar of soap and a mirror. This is where the workers "washed up" and combed their hair before entering the house for a meal. Farm and ranch work was not only hard, it was generally extremely dirty work!

Returning to the main course preparation, another memory I want to speak to is that Momma and I often butchered chickens for these work-crew meals. Chicken was prepared as either individually fried pieces or as chicken and dumplings—depending on the age of the chicken.

Now, if I were to really tell all of this chicken story, I would need to describe the chicken butchering process. For us, it began with having to—well—catch them first. We generally used a very efficient, long, lightweight pole with a stiff hook at the end. Almost foolproof. You could grab a chicken's leg right quick. One time, however, Momma had selected one particular older renegade hen who was not laying eggs—not earning her keep on our farm. She had flown the coop and was wild. It was my job to chase her down and catch her. I couldn't corner her alone, so my two brothers were called in to join in the chase. We finally had the hen squatted at the base of a small tree. My plan of action was to sneak up behind that tree and reach around with one arm and—well—I didn't see the old rusty nail sticking out of the tree trunk. I ripped a three-inch gash in my arm and we did have to make that long emergency trip into Fredericksburg to get it sewn up, plus a tetanus shot. Yes, we did catch that poor hen and she did eventually become the main ingredient in a huge pot of chicken and dumplings.

But my chicken butchering account is not yet complete. Once caught, the next phase required a sharp hatchet and a chopping block where you—well—you had to chop off the bird's head. I could go on to describe how you had to gut and clean out the innards. I could, but I won't gross out my tenderfoot readers. Unless you grew up on a farm or ranch, you simply cannot appreciate all the things we had to learn to do from "youngster-hood" on into adulthood. Odd thing is, I never thought there was anything unusual about any of this butchering stuff until I was married and moved away from "country life" in the 1950s.

For instance, at one point we were living in Temple, Texas. Our apartment was only one within two very large three-story apartment buildings that housed twelve married couples with children—the men all stationed in nearby Camp Hood. The tenants were our age, all college graduates, who were now in the military for their two year compulsory tour in the armed forces. These couples were all from back east, mostly New Yorkers. We were the only Texans in the entire complex.

Next door to our apartment was a Jewish couple with a small baby. One day, Ellen, a city girl, wanted to surprise her husband with a special dinner and she came to me, a country girl, asking for my help in that venture. She wanted to bake a whole chicken and make giblet gravy. I advised her to purchase her chicken whole and to cut up the giblets that usually came wrapped inside the chicken. I left her to cook. Before long came a knock on my door, telling me in a panic that she could not chop up all the giblets. When I got to her kitchen, I saw she was trying to cut up the neck!

With that bit of humor, I begin Chapter Six, sharing my chosen favorite main course recipes from the last sixty-plus years. You will find no lasagna, pizza, or highly unusual foods therein. I would describe all of my favorites as just plain simple, good, nutritious eating. All of the dishes have been tested, tasted, and tried and they have stood the assessment of quality. I have prepared them over and over because I know they will be pleasing to the people around my table. I guess I inherited that from my mother too—that meals served out of my kitchen must be good or they will never be presented on my table twice.

My recipes are grouped into beef, chicken, and pork and the final main course is a category all to itself—Grandma Sophie Durden's procedure in preparing her deliciously awesome Thanksgiving turkey and dressing.

Indoor Barbecued Brisket
from Ken and Barbara Peterman

Several years ago, our entire faculty and staff of our Comfort Elementary School was invited to Ken and Barbara's for a "beginning a new school year" dinner. They served this Bar-B-Q— the best I have ever eaten. Ken Peterman was the elementary school principal for many years.

Rub 2 tablespoons liquid smoke and salt on both sides of the brisket. Wrap in foil and refrigerate overnight. Next day, sprinkle onion and garlic salt on both sides, rewrap tightly and bake at 300-325 degrees for 5 hours. Remove from oven, cool completely, and refrigerate overnight. Slice thin, pour sauce over sliced brisket, rewrap and bake at 350 degrees for 30 minutes. Serve warm.

BBQ Sauce

1 1/2 tablespoons brown sugar
8 oz. catsup
1/4 cup water
1 tablespoon liquid smoke
2 tablespoons Worcestershire

1 1/2 tablespoons dry mustard
1 tablespoon celery seed
3 tablespoon butter
Salt and pepper to taste

Looking severely undernourished are the three Durden "boys."

No Peek Stew *by Dr. Joy Russell*

2 pkgs. beef stew meat, small pieces
1 box (2 pkgs.) onion soup mix
2 medium cans mushrooms
1 cup Mogen David grape wine
¹/₄ cup water
No salt, but pepper to taste

Place all ingredients in a Dutch oven and bake for 3 hours at 325 degrees. *Do not peek.* Serve over rice. A green salad and crusty rolls complete meal.

Swedish Meatballs

1 lb. ground beef
¹/₂ lb. ground lean pork
¹/₂ cup minced onion
³/₄ cup dry bread crumbs
1 tablespoon snipped parsley
2 teaspoons salt
¹/₈ teaspoon pepper
1 teaspoon Worcestershire
1 egg
¹/₂ cup milk
³/₄ cup salad oil

Mix thoroughly beef, pork, onion, bread crumbs, parsley, salt, pepper, Worcestershire sauce, egg, and milk. Refrigerate 2 hours. Shape mixture by rounded tablespoonfuls into balls. In large skillet, slowly brown and cook meatballs in oil. Remove meatballs and keep warm.

GRAVY
¹/₄ cup flour
1 teaspoon paprika
¹/₂ teaspoon salt
¹/₈ teaspoon pepper
2 cups hot water
³/₄ cup dairy sour cream

Blend together flour, paprika, salt, pepper. Brown in the left over oil in the meatball browning pan and slowly add hot water. Bring to a slow boil and reduce heat. Add sour cream and whisk until cream is dissolved into the gravy. Add meat balls and simmer on low heat for another 20-30 minutes. Serve hot with biscuits or crusty rolls.

> "I am not a glutton—I am an explorer of food."
> —ERMA BOMBECK (1927-1996)

Meat Loaf

(Double or triple recipes according to number of guests)

Our Episcopal church has a "once a month supper club" where members volunteer their homes for small group dinners in a party-like atmosphere—usually around a dozen people. The dinner parties are considered a ministry to welcome new members and generally intended to form "family relationships" within the congregation. The host house provides the main course and guests provide side dishes—sometimes suggested by the hostess to complete her menu. This main course meatloaf was served by Espie Faust and the recipe shared with me at my request. The recipe seems very routine but the taste is superb.

1½ pounds ground beef	¼ cup grated onion
2/3 cup dry bread crumbs	1 teaspoon salt
1 cup milk	½ teaspoon sage
2 beaten eggs	Dash of pepper

In a large bowl, soak bread crumbs in milk for 10 minutes, then add meat, eggs, onion, and seasonings. Mix well and place in a greased, glass 8½"×4½"×2½" loaf pan and bake at 350 degrees for one hour.

TOPPING:

3 tablespoons brown sugar	1 teaspoon dry mustard
¼ cup catsup	

Mix and spread on top of meat loaf the last 15 minutes of the baking time.

 A woman was trying hard to get the ketchup out of the jar. During her struggle the phone rang so she asked her 4-year-old daughter to answer the phone. "Mommy can't come to the phone to talk to you right now. She's hitting the bottle."

Meat Loaf
by Janis Schwab

Janis Schwab shared this recipe with me many years ago. Janis is the owner of Kountry Kurl, a Comfort beauty shop. She has appeared as Mrs. Santa Claus along side Mr. Claus in countless lighted night parades always held in Comfort on the Saturday following Thanksgiving—appropriately called CHRISTMAS IN COMFORT. This recipe, she told me, was the blue ribbon prizewinner at the Kendall County Fair during the 1980s. It is definitely a prizewinner.

1 1/2 lbs. hamburger
1 cup bread crumbs
1 egg, beaten
1 tablespoon chopped
   green pepper

2 tablespoons chopped onion
Salt and pepper to taste
1/2 can tomato sauce
1 teaspoon Worcestershire

Mix well and pack in loaf pan. Bake at 350 degrees for 1 1/2 hours. Baste with the following sauce from time to time during the baking process.

SAUCE:

1/2 can tomato sauce
1/2 can water
3 tablespoons brown sugar

1 tablespoon vinegar
1 teaspoon prepared mustard

Known around town as Mrs. Santa Claus, Janis Schwab appears alongside Santa every Saturday after Thanksgiving as the conclusion of a lighted night parade through the historic district of Comfort in an event called CHRISTMAS IN COMFORT.

If you're gonna live in Texas. . .
you gotta have a chili recipe in your file

Hearty Chili with Beans
Cozy, Comforting, Quick

1 pound lean ground beef
1 cup chopped onions
  (or more, to taste)
1 can (15.5 oz.) Ranch
  Style Beans (not drained)
1 can (15-oz.) diced tomatoes

1 package Pioneer Brand
  Chile mix
1 small can green chilis
  (your choice of heat)
1 cup water

Brown beef in a fry pan, add onions and cook 'til clear; put into a Dutch oven or crockpot. Add rest of ingredients to the selected pot and set on high temperature. Chili will be ready to serve in a few hours. Serve over regular sized Fritos, shredded sharp cheddar cheese, and finely chopped onion.

When we Texans fill out a table, there are three main dishes: meats, vegetables, and breads. We use three spices: salt, pepper, and ketchup! Oh, yeah ... We don't care what you folks in Cincinnati call that stuff you eat ... IT AIN'T REAL CHILI!!

Beef Casserole
*Make this just once and it will become
one of your favorite dishes*

1 cup uncooked elbow macaroni	1 tablespoon steak sauce
1 pound lean ground meat	Salt to taste
2 medium onions, diced	Pepper to taste
¹/₄ cup chopped green pepper	1 can cream of mushroom soup
1 can (15 oz.) diced tomatoes	1 cup grated cheese
2 tablespoons dried or	(sharp cheddar or
fresh parsley	monterey jack)
1 tablespoon ketchup	

Preheat oven to 350 degrees. Cook macaroni according to package directions.

Meanwhile, in a large skillet, brown ground beef. Add onion and green pepper and cook until onions are translucent. Add tomatoes, ketchup, steak sauce, and parsley. Cook 10 minutes. Stir in cooked and drained macaroni and season to taste with salt and pepper. Gently mix in cream of mushroom soup and transfer to casserole dish lightly sprayed with vegetable oil. Sprinkle cheese over top. Bake until casserole is bubbly and cheese is lightly browned, about 30 minutes. Makes 8 servings.

An "after golf" dinner honoring best friend and head librarian Irene Spenrath. From left to right: Curtis Voges, Martin Spenrath, Irene, Jerry Durden, Mae Durden, and Ramona Voges (back to camera). Missing golfer and taking picture was Rowena Chambers.

Spaghetti Pie

This came from my Superintendent's wife, Ginger Derr. She, Eddie Derr, and their three children loved this "family style" recipe. A definite keeper. I cut down the amount of spaghetti— my 9"×13" pan was not large enough to contain this original recipe. This is one of those recipes that has become a favorite for its ease of preparation—only a salad side is necessary to complete the meal.

1 pound ground lean beef
1 pound spaghetti
$^1/_2$ cup chopped onion
$^1/_2$ cup chopped green pepper
1 pint cottage cheese

4 ounces mozzarella cheese
$^1/_2$ cup parmesan cheese
2 tablespoon butter
2 well-beaten eggs
1 jar (32-oz.) Ragu sauce

Boil spaghetti according to directions. Drain. Add butter, eggs, and parmesan and spread evenly in bottom of a 13"×9" pan.

Cook onions and peppers until tender in small amount of oil. Add meat and brown. Add Ragu sauce. Heat thoroughly. Spread cottage cheese over spaghetti. Spread sauce mixture over cottage cheese. Add garlic and salt and pepper to taste. Bake 20 minutes at 375 degrees. Remove from oven and sprinkle grated mozzarella cheese over top. Return to oven until cheese melts. Remove from oven and let set for approximately 15 minutes. Cut into portions and serve with hot crusty rolls.

Chicken & Stuffing Skillet

1 tablespoon butter
4 boneless chicken
   breast halves
1 box (6-oz.) chicken flavor
   stuffing mix

1 can (10$^3/_4$ oz.) cream
   of mushroom soup
$^1/_2$ cup milk
$^1/_2$ cup shredded cheddar cheese

Heat butter in skillet. Add chicken and cook 12-15 minutes or until done. Remove chicken from pan and set aside.

Prepare stuffing in same skillet according to package directions except *don't let stand 2 minutes*. Top with chicken halves.

Mix soup and milk. Pour over chicken. Sprinkle with cheese. Cover and heat through. Serves 4.

Swiss Chicken Enchiladas
by Helen (Geistweidt) Hahn

If I were to say which is the one most favored main dish in my collection, without a doubt, it would have to be this one. The recipe is easy to assemble—is great tasting—and any leftovers freeze well and reheat wonderfully in a microwave. It came out of New Mexico from a great cook and my sister-in-law Helen Hahn.

1 can refried beans
1 dozen corn tortillas
1 can cream of chicken soup
1 soup can of water
1 cup chopped cooked
  boneless chicken

1 carton (8 oz.) sour cream
1 or 2 small cans chopped
  green chilies
1 1/2 cups grated sharp
  cheddar cheese

Spray 9"×13" baking dish with oil. Spread beans to cover bottom of pan. Place six tortillas over beans, overlapping evenly. Combine next five ingredients in large mixing bowl. Spread half of soup mixture over tortillas. Repeat with remaining tortillas and soup mixture. Sprinkle generously with grated cheese. Bake in 350-degree oven for 30-45 minutes.

King Ranch Tortilla Bake

*I think everyone in Texas has a favorite
King Ranch chicken recipe. This is mine.*

1 medium onion, chopped
1 tablespoon butter
1 can (10 oz.) cream of
  chicken soup
3/4 cup chicken broth
1 can black beans, drained

1 can (4 oz.) green chilies
12 tortillas
3 cups cooked chicken, shredded
2 cups shredded monterey
  jack cheese

In a large skillet, brown onion in butter until soft and translucent. In a medium bowl mix soup, broth, beans, and chilies. Add the soup/bean mixture to the browned onions in the skillet and heat through. In a 9"×13" greased casserole dish, place a layer of tortillas on the bottom. Spread a layer of chicken on top. Scoop the soup/bean mix on top of the chicken and layer with cheese. Repeat layers ending with cheese on top. Bake 30 minutes and serve.

Chicken Spaghetti

This recipe is from Cheryl Pomerenke, grill cook in Crawford, Texas. Crown Prince Abdullah of Saudi Arabia was a guest of President George W. Bush at his Crawford ranch and this dish was a favored one.

3 cups chicken	1 can (28-oz.) cream of
1 pkg. (12-oz.) thin spaghetti	chicken soup
3 tablespoons butter	1 cup milk
1/2 cup chopped celery	1 1/2 cups Velveeta
1/2 cup chopped onion	Salt and pepper to taste
1 tablespoon chopped pimento	Cheddar cheese, grated

Preheat oven to 350 degrees. In a large saucepan, cook chicken in boiling water until done. Drain, saving water. Add spaghetti to chicken water and cook until done according to directions on package. Chop chicken into small pieces. In another pan, melt butter and sauté celery and onion. Stir in pimento. Add chicken, soup, milk, Velveeta, salt, and pepper. Drain spaghetti and add to chicken mixture. Pour into 9"×13" baking dish and sprinkle cheddar. Bake for 20 minutes. Serves 8 to 10.

Cheesy Chicken Chowder

2 (14-oz.) cans chicken broth	1/4 cup butter
2 cups peeled, diced potatoes	1/3 cup flour
1 cup diced carrots	2 cups milk
1 cup diced celery	2 cups shredded
1/2 cup diced onion	cheddar cheese
1 teaspoon salt	2 cups diced or shredded
1/4 teaspoon pepper	cooked chicken

Bring chicken broth to a boil in a large saucepan. Reduce heat and add potatoes, carrots, celery, onion, salt, and pepper. Cover and simmer until vegetables are tender, about 15 minutes. Melt butter in a medium saucepan. Add flour and mix well. Gradually stir in milk and cook over low heat until slightly thickened. Stir in cheese and cook until melted. Add cheese mixture to broth and vegetables along with chicken. Cook and stir over low heat until thoroughly heated. Serves 8.

Hot Chicken Brunch Casserole

*This is a crunchy dish and is delicious
served inside puff pastries.*

4 chicken breasts	1 bay leaf
1 cup water	5 celery leaves

Simmer all together for 30 minutes. Set aside to cool.

2 cups celery, chopped	1 cup mayonnaise
1 cup water chestnuts, sliced	1 cup sour cream
$^1/_2$ cup mushrooms, sliced	2 tablespoons lemon juice
$^1/_2$ cup slivered almonds	Salt and pepper to taste
2 tablespoon minced onion	1 cup shredded cheddar cheese
$^1/_2$ can cream of chicken soup	1 cup French's fried onion rings

Mix all ingredients together. Chop cooled, drained chicken and toss in large bowl with above mixture. Spread into a 9"×13" baking dish. Top with cheese and French's onions. Bake in a 350 degree oven for 30 minutes. Serves 8-10.

World's Easiest Pot Pie *by Sieglinde Robinson*

This is Bill Nelson's favorite and I can't make it often enough to suit him. The recipe is out of a Travis County Homemakers Cookbook, a gift to me for being the guest speaker at a Tri-County luncheon of their Travis County Education Extension Associations. It was a great day for us. I am thankful and grateful to Violet Alexander for inviting us. You were a gracious host!

2 cans ($10^3/_4$ oz.) cream of potato soup	$^1/_2$ cup milk
	$^1/_2$ teaspoon thyme
1 (16 oz.) can mixed vegetables, drained	$^1/_2$ teaspoon black pepper
	2 pie crusts (9")
2 cups chicken or turkey cooked, diced	1 egg, beaten

Combine first 6 ingredients. Spoon into prepared unbaked pie crust. Cover with second crust, crimp edges to seal. Slit top crust and brush with beaten egg. Bake in preheated oven at 375 degrees for 40 minutes.

Baked Pork Chops
by Charlotte Holmes of Cypress Creek Inn

8 pork chops
Flour, as needed
1 onion, sliced
3 cups water

Dash of oregano
1 tablespoon catsup
2 bell peppers, chopped
Salt and pepper to taste

Mix flour, salt, and pepper and coat pork chops. Fry chops on both sides in shortening until lightly browned. Remove chops to a baking dish. In remaining pan shortening sauté onion, remove and drain. Add a bit of flour to the remaining shortening in fry pan and add 3 cups water to make gravy. Add oregano, catsup, bell peppers, salt and pepper to taste. Pour mixture over chops in baking dish. Bake at 400 degrees for one hour—turning chops twice during cooking time. Cover last 20 minutes so they won't burn.

Pork Chops with Vegetables

2 tablespoon oil
6 pork loin chops,
   ¹/₂ inch thick
1 green pepper, cut into strips
2 tablespoons flour
1 can condensed onion soup

2 tablespoon Worcestershire
1 teaspoon garlic powder
1 teaspoon salt
2 medium tomatoes,
   cut in wedges

Heat oil in large skillet. Three at a time, brown chops well on both sides. Remove and set aside. In remaining oil, add green pepper, sauté for three minutes, remove and set aside. Stir flour into frypan, cooking for one minute. Blend in soup, Worcestershire and seasonings. Bring to boiling point. Return chops to skillet; spoon sauce over chops. Cover and simmer until chops are tender, about one hour. Stir in tomatoes and the sautéed green pepper. Cover and simmer 5 minutes longer. Serves 6.

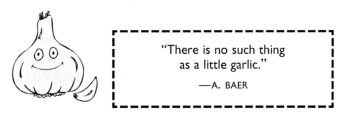

"There is no such thing
as a little garlic."

—A. BAER

Sweet and Sour Pork

1 pound pork loin
or boneless chops
3 tablespoons cornstarch
2 tablespoons brown sugar
2 tablespoons vinegar
2 tablespoons soy sauce
1 can (10¹/₂ oz.) beef
consommé

2 teaspoons vegetable oil
1 green pepper, cut into strips
1 sweet red pepper,
cut into strips
2 cloves of garlic, minced
1 can (20-oz.) pineapple
chunks, drained
4 cups hot cooked rice

Slice pork into very thin strips. Mix cornstarch, brown sugar, vinegar, soy, and consommé, set aside. Heat oil in skillet. Add pork and stir fry until brown. Remove pork. Add peppers and garlic to skillet and stir fry until tender crisp. Add pineapple. Stir in cornstarch mixture, cooking until mixture thickens, stirring constantly. Return pork to pan and heat thoroughly. Serve over rice. Serves 4.

Southern-Fried Pork Chops

6 center-cup pork chops,
¹/₂ inch thick
1 cup buttermilk
1 cup flour

1 teaspoon garlic powder
¹/₂ teaspoon pepper
1 teaspoon salt
Vegetable oil for frying

Pour oil in medium skillet, coating entire pan, medium high heat. Pour buttermilk into a shallow dish. In another dish, mix flour, garlic powder, pepper, and salt. Dip pork chops into buttermilk, then dredge in flour mix. Shake off excess flour and place in heated skillet. Cook until browned on one side. Turn and cook until done through. Serves 6.

Yum! I'm ready for dinner. How about you?

Pork Chops with Potatoes and Green Beans
by Katie Hahn

4-6 pork chops
1 tablespoon flour
4 medium potatoes, peeled,
   thinly sliced
10 oz. frozen green beans,
   French style

1 can cream soup
   (chicken or mushroom)
$^1/_4$ can water
Salt to taste
Paprika

Shake flour in empty brown-in-bag and place bag in pan. Season potatoes with salt and place in bag. Add green beans, partially thawed. Trim excess fat from pork chops. Sprinkle with salt and paprika and place on top of green beans. Pour soup and water over pork chops. Follow brown-in-bag instructions for cooking. Bake 1 hour.

One-Dish-Meal Taco Salad
by JoDell Hunt

This salad is actually a meal in one dish. It is unique in that all the ingredients can be prepared before hand, then "tossed together" in less than 5 minutes. It was an instant addition to my collection in the '70's when JoDell hosted a dinner with friends.

2 lbs. ground lean beef
1 can ranch-style beans,
   drained and rinsed
1-2 tablespoons chili powder
Lettuce, cut up
Tomatoes, fresh, cut up

Onions, cut up
Avocado, cut up
Cheese, hard, grated
2 lbs. Velveeta cheese
2 cans Rotel tomatoes
Fritos, 12-oz bag

Brown and set aside ground beef, beans, and chili powder.

Cut up and set aside in separate bowls in refrigerator: lettuce, fresh tomatoes, onions, avocado, and grated hard cheese.

Melt together in microwave: Velveeta cheese and Rotel tomatoes.

When ready to serve guests, toss together in a very large bowl: bag of Fritos, the lettuce mixture, and the meat mixture. Serve each guest a generous helping of this mixture. On buffet, place the hot cheese mixture along with a gravy ladle to self-serve as sauce.

Turkey & Dressing
The Grandma Sophie Durden Method

ONE DAY BEFORE your planned dinner, bake a double batch of plain cornbread. When baked, break it into medium sized pieces and leave on counter to dry out. On another plate, place five slices of day old bread to dry out.

EARLY NEXT DAY, chop 1 large onion; sauté in bacon grease. Meanwhile cut dry bread into small cubes and crumble up the dried out cornbread. Mix cornbread and bread together in large bowl and pour the cooked onion plus all the bacon grease over bread/cornbread. Toss together. Set aside. Cover lightly.

TURKEY—ALSO EARLY (6:00 a.m.) On the morning of a noon dinner, rub thawed turkey inside and outside with bacon grease and pepper. No salt. Place turkey (breast side down) in a large deep roaster and pour hot boiling water to just cover the bottom of the roaster. Cover and place in a 275-325 degree oven. Keep temperature even and don't open roaster for four hours. After four hours, remove roaster cover and begin to baste turkey with pan drippings. Add a little more hot water to drippings. Do not turn turkey, leave on breast. Continue to baste every 20 minutes with pan drippings until fifteen minutes before carving and serving time. Remove turkey from oven to "rest"—leave turkey on breast.

DRESSING: While turkey is baking, fry the finely chopped giblets (heart and liver) in bacon grease. Pour over dried out bread/cornbread/onion mixture. Also add two slightly beaten eggs, 2 cups finely chopped celery, 1 tablespoon poultry seasoning, 1 teaspoon salt, and a dash of pepper. Dissolve three chicken bouillon cubes in 1 1/2 cups boiling water and pour over cornbread/bread/onion mixture—moisten to good handling consistency. Mix and toss with hands, kneading lightly and pack loosely into loaf pans small enough to fit into the oven beside turkey. Begin baking 1 hour before serving time. (Should be crusty on top after baking.)

GRAVY: Once turkey baking is completed and bird is put onto large carving platter, gravy will be made from the roaster drippings by simply mixing flour with cold water (paste) and gradually adding that to the boiling drippings. Add more water and seasoning if desired. (This recipe based on a 15-20 pound turkey.)

CHAPTER SEVEN

Side Dishes

Hot German Potato Salad
by Susan Rose Durden

This recipe came to me from my daughter-in-law. If you fix this and can find one person who does not love this taste—well—I won't believe you!

5 lbs. potatoes	1 bottle capers and juice
1 medium onion, chopped	1/2 cup white vinegar
4-5 slices bacon	Salt and pepper to taste
3/4 cup sugar	

Boil, peel, and dice potatoes and set aside. Fry onion and bacon (cut into small strips) until browned. Stir in sugar, capers and juice, white vinegar, salt, and pepper. Stir till sugar dissolves and pour mixture over diced potatoes. Mix well. Cover with foil and keep warm in oven.

Potato Casserole

2 lbs. thawed hash browns	1/2 onion, finely chopped
1 stick butter, melted (divided use)	10 oz. grated sharp cheddar
	1 teaspoon salt
2 cups sour cream	1/2 teaspoon pepper
1 can cream of mushroom soup	2 cups cornflakes

Heat oven to 350 degrees. Grease 9"×13" baking dish. Mix hash browns, 1/2 stick butter, sour cream, soup, onion, cheese, salt, and pepper. Put into prepared baking dish. Top with corn flakes mixed with remaining butter. Bake for 45 minutes. 12 servings.

Potato Supreme

5 large baking potatoes,
  boiled and sliced
2 cups evaporated milk
1 stick butter
1 tablespoon salt

$^1/_2$ lb. Velveeta cheese
1 sour cream (8 oz.)
8 slices bacon, cooked until
  crisp and crumbled
8 green onions, chopped

Preheat oven to 350 degrees. Prepare potatoes. Place into greased 9"×13" pan. Set aside.

In saucepan, combine milk, butter, salt, and cheese. Heat until butter and cheese melt. Pour over potatoes to cover completely. Bake about 40 minutes. Remove from oven, spread sour cream on top of hot potatoes. Sprinkle with bacon and green onions.

Coconut–Crumble Sweet Potato

2 eggs
3 cups cooked, mashed
  sweet potato (or
  40-oz. canned)
$^1/_2$ cup sugar
$^1/_4$ cup sweetened
  condensed milk

$^2/_3$ cup butter, melted
  (divided use)
1 teaspoon vanilla
1 cup flaked coconut
1 cup packed dark
  brown sugar
$^1/_3$ cup flour

Preheat oven to 375 degrees. Grease 8" square baking dish.

Place eggs in large bowl. Beat well. Add sweet potatoes, sugar, condensed milk, $^1/_3$ cup butter, and vanilla. Mix well and spoon into baking dish. Combine coconut, brown sugar, flour, and remaining butter in a medium bowl. Stir until well blended and sprinkle over potato mixture. Bake uncovered 35-45 minutes until top is golden brown and knife inserted into center comes out clean. Let stand 15 minutes before serving. Serves 8-10.

> "People who like to cook like to talk about food ... without one cook giving another cook a tip or two, human life might have died out a long time ago."
>
> —LAURIE COLWIN, *Home Cooking*

Corn Pudding
by Charlotte Holmes and Cypress Creek Inn

1 can creamed corn
$^1/_2$ cup bread crumbs
$^1/_2$ teaspoon salt
2 eggs, lightly beaten

$^3/_4$ cup milk
1 tablespoon sugar
2 tablespoons melted butter

Mix all ingredients together. Pour in greased loaf pan. Sprinkle top with paprika. Bake at 350 degrees about 1 hour or until set.

Canned Corn Casserole

1 can (15-oz.) whole
kernel corn, drained
1 can (15-oz.) cream
style corn
1 box Jiffy Corn Muffin mix

$^1/_2$ cup sugar
2 eggs, well beaten
1 stick butter, melted
1 cup sour cream

Preheat oven to 350 degrees. Mix together all ingredients in a bowl. Pour into a well-greased 9"×13" baking dish. Bake 45-60 minutes until center is firm.

Green Bean Casserole

8 cups cooked French-cut
green beans
$^1/_2$ onion, finely grated
2 cans ($10^3/_4$ oz.) cream of
mushroom soup

1 cup milk
2 teaspoons soy sauce
1 teaspoon black pepper
1 can (6-oz.) French Fried
Onion rings

Stir soup, milk, soy sauce, black pepper, grated onion, beans, 1 and $^1/_3$ cups French Fried onions in a 3 quart casserole. Bake at 350 degrees for 25 minutes. Stir. Top with remaining F.F. onions. Bake 5 minutes more. 12 servings.

Laughter is brightest where food is best."
—IRISH PROVERB

Five-a-Day Vegetables with Parmesan Cheese

4 cups thinly sliced zucchini
1 small onion, sliced
1 green or yellow bell pepper,
  cut into strips
1 medium carrot, grated
1 tablespoon water
2 tablespoons butter

1 teaspoon salt
Black pepper, to taste
1 1/4 teaspoons Italian seasoning
1 cup diced fresh tomatoes,
  seeds removed
1/4 cup grated parmesan cheese

Combine zucchini, onion, bell pepper, carrot, water, butter, salt, pepper, and Italian seasoning in a large skillet. Cover and cook 1 minute. Uncover and continue to cook, turning with a wide spatula, until veggies are crisp-tender, 5-15 minutes. Add tomatoes and parmesan cheese. Toss and cook another minute. Serves 8-10

Texas Squash

8 yellow squash, sliced
1 tablespoon grated onion
2 cups Fritos,
  coarsely crushed

1 cup grated sharp
  cheddar cheese
1/4 cup (1/2 stick) butter, melted
1 can chopped green chilies

Cook sliced squash for 5 minutes in salted water to cover. Drain and use spoon to coarsely mash squash; do not over mash. Add remaining ingredients to squash, toss and place in greased casserole dish. Bake in preheated oven 325 degrees for 30 minutes or until heated throughout.

Chisom Durden communicating with his Grandpa Jerry over food, of course.

Homesteader's Four-Bean Casserole

8 bacon slices
3 to 4 medium onions, cut
    into rings and separated
$^1/_2$ to $^3/_4$ cup maple syrup or
    packed dark brown sugar
1$^1/_2$ teaspoons garlic powder
1 teaspoon dry mustard
$^1/_4$ cup apple cider vinegar

1 can (15 oz.) dark red kidney
    beans (drained)
1 can (15 oz.) lima beans,
    drained
1 can (16 oz.) butter beans,
    drained
1 can (16 oz.) baked beans,
    undrained

Cook bacon in large skillet over medium/high heat until crisp. Remove and drain on paper towels; crumble and set aside.

Add onions, syrup, garlic powder, and dry mustard to pan drippings. Reduce heat to medium and add vinegar, taking care because steam will rise. Cover and cook 20 minutes. Preheat oven to 350 degrees. Grease 9"×13" baking dish. Add beans to pan. Stir in onion mixture and bacon; mix well. Cover and bake 45 minutes. Remove from oven, uncover, and let stand 20-25 minutes before serving. Serves 12.

Hoppin' John (Black-eyed Peas)

1 tablespoon olive oil
1 medium onion, diced
1 red bell pepper, diced
2 garlic cloves, minced
2 cans (15-oz.) black-eyed
    peas, rinsed and drained

$^1/_4$ cup water
1 teaspoon salt
$^1/_2$ teaspoon pepper
2 green onions, thinly sliced
$^1/_4$ cup finely minced parsley

Heat olive oil in a large saucepan over medium heat. Add onion, red bell pepper, and garlic. Sauté until onions are translucent, about 5 minutes. Stir in peas, water, salt, and pepper. Reduce heat to low; cook 10 more minutes. Stir in green onions and parsley. Serves 6.

> The first zucchini I ever saw I killed it with a hoe."
> —JOHN GOULD, *Monstrous Depravity* (1963)

Boston Baked Beans *by Anita Rhodes*

A wonderful old-fashioned baked bean flavor. This recipe has served my family for 29 years and originally came from my mother-in-law. It tastes great served with fresh cornbread or biscuits and honey. Although you need to allow time for soaking and simmering the beans, this recipe is still quite easy.

3²/₃ cups dry navy beans
16 oz. bacon
1¹/₂ onion, finely diced
¹/₃ cup molasses
1 tablespoon plus
　³/₄ teaspoons salt
¹/₂ teaspoon black pepper

¹/₂ teaspoon dry mustard
³/₄ cup plus 2 tablespoons
　plus 2 teaspoons ketchup
1 tablespoon and 2¹/₂ teaspoons
　Worcestershire
¹/₃ cup plus 2 tablespoons
　brown sugar

Soak beans overnight in cold water. Simmer beans in same water until tender, approximately 1-2 hours. Drain and reserve liquid. Preheat oven to 325 degrees. Arrange beans in a 2-quart bean pot or casserole dish by placing a portion of the beans in the bottom of the dish, and layering them with bacon and onion. In a saucepan, combine rest of ingredients. Bring mixture to a boil and pour over the beans. Pour in just enough of the bean water to cover the beans. Cover dish with a lid or foil. Bake for 3-4 hours in preheated oven, until beans are tender. Remove lid about halfway through cooking, and add more liquid if necessary to prevent beans from getting too dry. Serves 12.

Po Po Restaurant's Pickled Beets

1 (14.5-oz.) can small beets
　(not pickled)
1 cup sugar
¹/₄ cup apple cider vinegar

¹/₃ teaspoon cinnamon
¹/₃ teaspoon cloves
¹/₄ onion, coarsely chopped

Drain and discard the juice from beets and place in a bowl. In a pan, combine sugar, vinegar, cinnamon, cloves, and onion. Bring to a boil and cook briefly, stirring to dissolve the sugar. Pour over beets; let cool, then cover and refrigerate one day before serving. Serve chilled.

Simi's Cabbage

1 pound green cabbage	$^1/_2$ cup chopped onion
(about $^1/_2$ small head)	$^1/_4$ teaspoon turmeric
2-3 tablespoon vegetable oil	1 medium tomato, diced
4 cloves garlic, finely chopped	$^1/_2$ cup frozen peas
$^1/_2$ tablespoon finely grated ginger	Salt to taste
$^3/_4$ teaspoon cumin	

Cut cabbage into 1-inch pieces and set aside. Heat vegetable oil in a large skillet over medium heat. Add garlic, ginger, and cumin; cook briefly, stirring constantly, just until the garlic begins to brown. Add the cabbage and onion, cook about 30 seconds, then add the turmeric. Stir and fry the mixture for about 5 minutes, then add the tomato and peas. Continue cooking and stirring until cabbage is crisp/tender. Season to taste with salt. Serves 4.

Just a word about cabbage. It could be a German cultural thing, but I love to simply chop cabbage and steam it in a Teflon fry pan w/enough water to steam until it is lightly browned. I add a bit of salt and pepper and I have a low/no calorie side dish. Needs lots of attention during cooking.

Cranberry Crunch *by Susan Rose Durden*

This recipe is from my daughter-in-law. She brought it to one of our Durden family Christmas gatherings. It's different, pretty and very good!

1 cup oatmeal	6 tablespoons butter, melted
$^1/_2$ cup flour	1 can (whole berry)
$^1/_3$ cup brown sugar	cranberry sauce
$^1/_2$ cup coconut	Pecans, chopped

Mix first five ingredients until moistened. Layer: first with 1 can whole berry cranberry sauce, then crumbly mixture, sauce and mixture. Sprinkle with pecans and bake at 350 degrees for about 30 minutes or until lightly browned and bubbly.

(Susan multiplied this recipe three times to serve our large family group).

Broccoli Casserole

1 onion, chopped	1 small can sliced mushrooms,
3 tablespoons butter	drained
3 (10-oz.) frozen,	$^1/_3$ cup blanched almonds
chopped broccoli	$^1/_2$ cup bread crumbs
1 can cream of mushroom soup	2 tablespoons butter
1 (6-oz.) roll garlic cheese	

Sauté onion in 3 tablespoon butter. Add broccoli and cook until separated, then add soup, cheese, and mushrooms. Put in ungreased casserole and sprinkle with almonds, then bread crumbs. Top with the 2 tablespoons butter. Bake in 350 degree oven for 30-40 minutes.

Broccoli and Grape Salad *by Molly Houck*

Molly Houck got it from the NM Cumbres & Toltec Scenic Railroad Cookbook. *Yumm.*

1 bunch broccoli, cut into	1 bunch red seedless grapes
bite-size pieces	$^1/_2$ cup sliced green onion

Combine broccoli and grapes in a bowl and add green onions.

DRESSING:

1 cup mayonnaise	$^1/_2$ cup sunflower seeds
2 tablespoons vinegar	$^1/_2$ cup real bacon bits
$^1/_3$ cup sugar	

In a separate bowl mix dressing ingredients well. Pour over prepared salad and add bacon bits and sunflower seeds just before serving.

Cats do not like broccoli—
but they mind their
mommas!

Heloise's Mother's Pickled Beets

3 (16-oz.) cans beets,
  sliced or whole
1 cup sugar
1 cup vinegar
2 tablespoons cornstarch

24 whole cloves, fewer to taste
3 tablespoons ketchup
3 tablespoons oil (optional)
1 teaspoon vanilla
Salt to taste

Drain beets, reserving 1½ cups of the beet liquid. Place beets in a medium saucepan with the reserved liquid and the remaining ingredients. Mix well, then cook for three minutes over medium heat or until the mixture thickens. Let cool and refrigerate.

Bourbon Pickled Apricots or Peaches

1 cup cider vinegar
1 cup orange juice
½ cup white grape juice
¼ cup sugar
¼ cup maple syrup
2 teaspoons whole
  allspice berries

8 whole cloves
Zest of 2 oranges
1 tablespoon minced ginger
8 apricots (quartered, pitted),
  or 8 medium peaches, peeled,
  quartered, and pitted
¼ cup bourbon

In a non-reactive saucepan, combine vinegar, orange juice, grape juice, sugar, and maple syrup; bring to boil over high heat, stirring occasionally to dissolve sugar. Add allspice and cloves. As soon as mixture comes back to boil, reduce to low and simmer 5 minutes. Remove from heat; add zest and ginger. Cool to room temperature. Add apricots or peaches and bourbon; gently toss. Spoon into canning jars and seal. Refrigerate at least 2 days or up to 6 weeks. Serves with pork chops, ham, or ribs.

Pickled beets are a treat anytime!

Cranberry Relish Mold

1 (#2 can) crushed pineapple
2 pkgs. Cherry Jell-O
3/4 cup sugar
2 cups hot water
1/2 cup cold water
1 or 2 tablespoons
    lemon juice

1 1/2 cups ground raw
    cranberries (about 1 pound)
1 small orange (ground
    with cranberries)
1 cup chopped celery
1/4 cup pecans, chopped

Drain pineapple, save juice. Combine Jell-O and sugar and dissolve in the hot water. Add cold water, lemon juice and saved pineapple juice. Chill until partially set. Add pineapple, other ingredients, and pour into 2 quart mold. Refrigerate over night. 12 servings.

Combination Bean Salad

16 oz. can cut green
    beans, drained
16-oz. can yellow wax
    beans, drained
15-oz. can red kidney beans,
    drained and rinsed

1 medium sliced onion
1 green pepper, sliced
3/4 cup sugar
1/2 cup apple cider vinegar
1/2 cup salad oil

Combine beans, onion, and pepper, set aside. Mix in a jar: sugar, vinegar, and salad oil; seal jar. Shake until sugar is mostly dissolved and pour over the bean mixture. Place in a glass bowl with cover and refrigerate at least one hour. Best refrigerated overnight and served next day.

This recipe is from the *Fredericksburg Home Kitchen Cook Book*, ninth edition, published by the Fredericksburg Parent-Teacher Association submitted by Mrs. Allen Keller.

"After a good dinner, one can forgive anybody,
even one's relatives."
—OSCAR WILDE

Shoepeg Salad *by Mary Sansom*

1 can (16 oz.) green beans, French cut, drained
1 can (16 oz.) LeSeur green peas, drained
1 can (12 oz.) white shoepeg corn, drained

1 jar (12 oz.) diced pimento, drained
1 cup chopped celery
1/2 cup purple or white onion, chopped
1 bell pepper, chopped

Combine the above ingredients in a large bowl. Set aside.

In a medium saucepan, mix 1/2 cup sugar, 1/2 cup oil, 1/2 cup apple cider vinegar, 1 garlic clove (diced), 1 teaspoon salt and 1/2 teaspoon pepper. Bring to a boil to dissolve sugar. Cool. Pour over combined vegetables and chill well. Refrigerate overnight.

Tomato Aspic *by Sarah (Nelson) Crawford*

Bill Nelson's mother's recipe. Bill says, "We always had it at Thanksgiving and Christmas. It is still a Nelson family favorite, a tradition."

2 pkgs. Lemon Jell-O
1 can tomato soup
1 can stewed tomatoes, drain and set aside liquid

1/2 cup pecans, chopped
1/2 cup celery, chopped
1/2 cup plain olives, chopped

In a medium saucepan, over medium heat, mix Jell-O in the drained-off liquid from stewed tomatoes. Then, add enough water to make two cups. Bring to boil, then stir until Jell-O is dissolved. Add the other ingredients, mix well. Place in favorite serving dish, cool and refrigerate overnight.

"Those magazine dieting stories always have the testimonial of a woman who wore a dress that could slipcover New Jersey in one photo and thirty days later looked like a well-dressed thermometer."

—ERMA BOMBECK (1927-1996)

Spinach Salad

1 package fresh raw	¹/₄ pound fresh mushrooms,
baby spinach	sliced
2-3 hard boiled eggs	10 strips bacon,
1 large onion, cut and	fried and crushed
separated into rings	

Toss all together in large glass bowl. Set aside.

DRESSING:

³/₄ cup sugar	1 cup white vinegar
¹/₂ cup oil	1 teaspoon salt

Place dressing ingredients in glass jar, seal and shake to dissolve sugar. Just before serving, pour dressing over salad and toss.

Entertaining with an open house was a special day when University of Texas Professor of Germanic Studies Dr. Hans Boas spent all day with the Nelsons interviewing Comfort citizens who still speak German. Dr. Boas founded the Texas German Dialect Project and has interviewed some 380 speakers of "Texas" German. The project is looking for old pictures, diaries, letters, newspapers, minutes of church meetings, or any other type of document that helps us understand what Texas German life was like in the nineteenth and early twentieth centuries. Pictured from left to right are Leslie Pressler, Ed and Sylvia Albrecht, and Dr. Boas. The two with backs to the camera are unknown.

Sweet Rice (Suszer Reis)
An old traditional German recipe.

1 cup rice
2 cups whole milk
¹/₂ cup sugar, or more to taste

1 tablespoon butter
Sugar and cinnamon

Cook rice according to package directions. Add milk, sugar, and butter and simmer slowly for about 20-30 minutes. Stir often to prevent sticking. Place in serving dish and sprinkle liberally with sugar and cinnamon. May be served hot or cold.

Sauerkraut (Pickled Cabbage)

This is another one of those recipes so traditional in German pioneer households. I can remember my Momma did this one year when we had a bumper crop of cabbage out of our garden. Since this is a dish still served up on most German tables, this book would not be complete without this recipe on how to make sauerkraut.

Choose only firm and fresh white cabbage. Remove the outer leaves and shred finely. (Ho'bel was what we called the shredder). Pack alternate layers of shredded cabbage and salt into a crock pressing down firmly so that the juice will cover the cabbage. (Salt will draw juice from the cabbage.) Cover the top layer with several cabbage leaves, then a board, and then a weight (a heavy stone, heavy enough to make the brine come up to the board.) Cover the crock with a piece of cloth secured with a string and store in a cool place. Time for fermentation is from four to six weeks.

Sauerkraut and sausage—
best home cooking ever!

Mixed Pickles by Clara E. Hahn

This is the recipe Momma used every summer for one of my family's favorite side dishes. Sealed in jars, we could have it throughout the winter. I remember washing pint jars for canning this condiment. I loved to watch when she added the turmeric and the entire mixture turned bright yellow.)

Finely cut up cabbage, thinly slice young cucumbers, young green beans (cut into 1 inch pieces), thinly sliced small green tomatoes, and cauliflower cut into bite size bites. Toss all together and sprinkle with salt and let stand over night. Drain and boil in weak vinegar water for 10 minutes. Add to mixture: 2 cups vinegar, 2 cups sugar, 1/2 cup flour, and 1 tablespoon turmeric. Mix all and let come to a boil until veggies are tender. Fill into jars, seal while hot.

Pea Salad

This dish was brought to my Mom and Dad's 25th wedding anniversary celebration in 1945. Drain a can of peas. Dice some yellow cheese, onion, and pimento and mix everything with mayonnaise and a dash of chili powder and salt to taste.

Pie Melon

A wonderful side dish throughout the winter months.

Pie melons were grown in our field and in the fall the entire family sat around our dinner table and picked out the tiny black seeds. Then Momma cut the melon into 1/4 inch strips. Cooked the next day, she used this formula: 7 lbs. melon to 3 lbs. sugar and 1/4 cup vinegar. Cook until syrup is thick and seal while hot into quart jars.

"One of the delights of life is eating with friends, second to that is talking about eating. And, for an unsurpassed double whammy, there is talking about eating while you are eating with friends."

—LAURIE COLWIN, *Home Cooking*

CHAPTER EIGHT

Bread and Muffins

It came as a complete surprise! I spread out my own collected bread recipes and found no regular bread recipe for this book. I then scoured my mother's old recipes—there was naught about Momma's wonderful daily bread. Impossible. She baked bread every day when all five of her children were still at home. I watched her. I agonized about this matter but I soon realized that there was no written recipe because she didn't need one. As I think back, I also remember that she made her own yeast cakes. I watched that process too and there's no recipe in her collection.

So what can I say other than that my mother's homemade bread was the best I have ever tasted. It had a wonderful texture inside and was pleasingly crusty on the outside. As to how she accomplished that, I can only try to remember her routine: I know she began by setting her yeast in warm water; a little later she'd mix a certain amount of water and flour into that and she'd leave it for a little while inside the old wood stove warmer space. Some time later, she sifted a large amount of flour into a very large glazed porcelain bowl then added the warm yeast mixture to it, along with some lard, and a little bit of salt and sugar, and with her large spoon she mixed and mixed and mixed until it could not be stirred any longer. She then sifted out a large amount of flour directly onto the small table in the corner of our tiny kitchen, dumped the flour/yeast glob onto that flour, and then she'd go to work kneading and kneading and kneading until the glob of dough looked all shiny and elastic. She then placed that glob back into the same bowl, now greased with lard, and finally she covered it with a kitchen towel and set it near the wood stove to rise. An hour or so later, we'd be back in the kitchen; the dough had doubled in size. Momma'd punch it down and the dough would shrink down to half its size in volume. At this point, we each greased our hands, pulled a small glob off the dough and shaped it into loaves and placed them in two greased black 8"×4"×4" bread baking pans. We then shaped three more loaves but placed them side by side, (rubbing each side with lard where they would touch), into one larger black 15"×9"×4" deep bread pan.

Now, those loaves had to rise again. When they had risen enough—like one inch or more above the rim of the pans, Momma'd carefully slide all into the oven she had preheated with the correct amount of wood for the correct bread baking temperature. Thirty or so minutes later, the most wonderful aroma of freshly baked bread permeated the entire house.

I cannot recall that mom ever burned her bread. Some people might not find this remarkable. I am totally blown away by all the innate abilities of our pioneer cooks. Consider also, all the while they labored, they exuded a constant strong hard-working positive persona—she kept her family fed and clothed and generally made her children feel hopeful for the future. At least, it was so in my family. As I grow older, I appreciate that more and more.

To enhance and support what I have just written, I recall my first meeting with my publisher, Ed Eakin, the owner of Eakin Press in Austin, Texas (now Waco). This was in 1998 after my retirement from elementary library. I'd been widowed in 1994 and had since married a longtime friend, Bill Nelson. I immediately set about trying to write. Subsequently, I submitted for publication to Eakin Press my first attempt at a book length manuscript entitled *I Just Called Her Momma*. Three weeks later, Mr. Eakin telephoned to express an interest in my book. Bill and I met at his office to discuss publication. During this meeting Mr. Eakin remembered another book he'd recently published that was also about Germans in Texas. He handed me a book entitled *Rezepte—German-Texan Culinary Art* written by Nevilee Maass Weaver and he insisted I take the book as a gift from him. I brought it home, glanced through it, smiled knowingly at its contents, and placed the tome on my book shelf. It remained there, unread until about twenty minutes ago, when I was deep into writing this narrative about my mother and her bread baking. I retrieved Weaver's book.

Bizarre! Ms. Weaver's publication is a treasure trove collection of recipes—originally written in German. They were given to her in 1976 from her aunt who gave them to Weaver for translation and preservation for the family. All of the recipes go back to pioneer days. I quote from her preface: "Now that this collection of heritage recipes is available to be explored and enjoyed, I ask that it be passed onto the next generation. A fragment of our Texan-German heritage will then be preserved."

I continued to browse through the book. I found on page 60: "A Good Recipe for Yeast: Shell 2 ears good, dry corn. Wash corn kernels in cold water, then pour $1^{1}/_{2}$ quarts of boiling water over it and cook until the corn is soft. More water may be needed during boiling. Let the water and corn cool until you can comfortably hold a finger in it. Pour the water in a big pan. Discard the cooked corn kernels. One must make the yeast cakes on the day that bread is to be baked, so that one can take out a pint of bread dough and mix with cornmeal and the corn water. Use enough cornmeal to make dough stiff enough to form cakes with hands. This yields about 21 yeast cakes, let it dry in the air. It's best to wrap them in paper. When yeast cakes made in this way are used, good bread is always the result." I saw my mom do exactly that! Bizarre how things come together.

Hence, let us go back now to our own farmhouse kitchen. I want to insert that some time later on, my mother bought a bread maker. No. Not like today's electric bread makers. This was a kind of bucket (for want of a better word) that she could clamp/hook/fasten onto her kitchen table. It

An authentic antique Bread Bucket, showing the dough hook and all the parts vital to the homemade bread baker. A bucket of this sort was recently spotted on eBay at a handsome cost.

had a dough hook that was hand turned with a large handle. I can't remember if

that did away with the floury mess left on the table after the kneading phase of bread making. I do remember that her yeast cake making was eventually replaced by "dry yeast" available in grocery
stores.

Moving on from this chapter's introduction—to telling about
Momma's bread making method—to reading parts of Ms. Weaver's
book on old time recipes—suddenly—out of the blue—my memory did an interesting flip-flop. It came to me as a "light-flash-
above-the-head" moment—my sister-in-law, Lillian Hahn, still occasionally bakes bread. She is 83. If I could put a loaf of her bread
and a loaf of my Momma's bread side by side, there would be no
difference. Furthermore, having had the enjoyable experience of
tasting Lillian's bread—God bless her!—her bread is my mother's
bread clone. As quickly as I could, I got in touch with Lillian and
as it turns out—well—this is the story as it was told to me:

Even though her bread baking education began in her teens
helping her mother, Lillian (Land) Hahn's serious bread baking
began after she married my brother, Otto Hahn in 1947. It was
only natural that she should continue to use her mother's method.
Her mother, Mrs. Hedwig (Wilke) Land, got her method from her
mother, and in all probability, the method goes back even further.
And, likewise, talking about yeast, Lillian said she remembers her
mother, Hedwig, making her own up until the time of dry yeast.

But, the story continues! Cindee Bohnert, Lillian's oldest
daughter, also began to bake bread in 1970 when she married.
Cindee however broke the current "method means" to bread baking by asking her Oma, Mrs. Land, for her recipe. Like so many
cooks of that era, Oma's measurements were by "gut denken."
Carefully watching her grandmother, Cindee found that Oma used
"handfuls" as her measurement for the flour. Working with her
grandmother, they actually determined her bread making ingredient measurements, adjusted them from experience, and finally the
recipe was written down.

Cindee continued her bread-making activities even while she
was a busy wife and professional office manager for her husband
Bill's growing business. She raised three children—two sons,
Robert, now 28, and Neal, now 31, and one daughter, Jessica, now
29. Cindee's energy astounds in that when Jessica recently married,

she and Jessica baked all the bread for her reception. In preparation, Cindee used a guide and figured they would get 13 slices per loaf. Between mother and daughter, they baked a total of 40+ loaves in 12 baking sessions. They happily tell the story that there were a few loaves left after the reception and when Uncle Warren Hahn asked what they was going to do with the leftover bread, Cindee gave him a loaf as a "party favor." It was not long before word got around to the remaining guests and she quickly ran out of bread. (Robert's wedding rehearsal dinner also featured Cindee's bread.)

And, yes. Jessica bakes bread regularly now too. I asked Jessica if any of her friends bake bread. "No, they don't, but they sure like to eat it and they are always asking me to share my baked bread with them." When asked if she ever used an electric bread maker, Jessica replied, "No, I don't. We got one as a wedding present but I prefer to use Oma's recipe. I enjoy baking, especially since my husband, Lance Elliott, really likes it. He was not used to eating homemade bread."

Jessica has been employed at Dutchmen's Market in Fredericksburg for the past twelve years. She also bakes sweet rolls—something her colleagues are forever asking for. Her recipe? "I use Oma's recipe." Jessica is also a busy wife and mother of two sons, Cody and Jacob.

I asked Lillian if her family ever calls her asking for her recipes. That question elicited a hearty laugh, "Well, yes! Heather even called me for my recipe for pot roast. She lives in Florida!" (Heather is another granddaughter.)

Jessica suddenly broke out in laughter. "I was just remembering when I baked bread for the first time—or rather, when I tried. My cousin, Carrie Oestreich, was spending the night with me. After everybody had gone to bed, Carrie and I decided to bake some bread. We were like ten or eleven at the time. We mixed up this dough but didn't use enough water or something and we ended up with a really big mess."

Cindee chimed in, "Yeah, and the next morning we found all these little globs of dough balls all over the kitchen!"

The laughter that followed rang with affection and solid friendships between grandmother, daughter, and granddaughter. The baking of bread or just sharing kitchen times together always seems

to generate solid strong relationships. As with these three generations of daughters, it seems evident that the leavening agent at work
here is love. *Salute!*

Oma's Homemade Bread
from Lillian's mother Mrs. Harry Land

2 packages dry yeast   5 tablespoons sugar
1 quart lukewarm water   8 tablespoon shortening, melted
2 tablespoons salt   11 cups flour (approximately)

Dissolve yeast in lukewarm water. Add sugar, salt and shortening. Add 2 to 3 cups flour, stir well. Continue adding flour until un-
able to stir. Begin to knead, adding flour as needed until smooth
and dough cleans sides of bowl and is not sticky to the touch. Cover
and let rise until double in size. Punch down and let rise until double in size again. Punch down and divide into 3 equal portions.
Shape into loaves and place into 3 greased loaf pans. Let rise. Bake
at 350 degrees for 1 hour.

Four generations of avid homemade bread bakers using the original recipe, Oma's Homemade
Bread. Inset photo is Hedwig (Wilke) Land (deceased), the mother of the woman in the center,
Lillian (Land) Hahn, who is the mother of the woman on her left, Cindee (Hahn) Bohnert, who is
the mother of the young woman on Lillian's right, Jessica (Bohnert) Elliott. The bread on the table
is Oma's recipe.

Events such as this have permeated my writing career for the past fourteen years. It is what make this activity so much fun. For instance, yesterday Bill Nelson's daughter came for a visit. In telling her my sister-in-law's story, Martha began to tell about how she remembers her own mother (Kit) also baking bread. Martha added, "I can still see her turning the handle of a bread bucket and . . ." (Kit, Bill's deceased wife of 46 years was a personal friend of mine.) Whereupon, Bill searched for and found Kit's recipe.

Good Wheat Bread *by Kit Nelson*

1 pkg. dry yeast
$1^1/2$ cups warm water
1 small can evaporated milk
$^1/2$ cup safflower oil

$^1/2$ cup honey
2 eggs, slightly beaten
$3^1/2$ cups whole wheat flour
$3^1/2$ cup unbleached flour

Dissolve yeast in water. Add milk, oil, honey, and eggs. Add flours gradually until dough cannot be stirred by hand. Knead adding flours until desired consistency. Place in oiled pan to rise until double in size. Shape into 3 loaves and place into greased pans. Let rise. Bake at 350 degrees for 30 minutes.

Good, wholesome
wheat bread

The Search Continues

As I continued to search through my mother's recipes, I found many old tattered recipes using Robin Hood Flour printed alongside Betty Crocker's face. How impressed we were with that name—which led me to research the Internet—to refresh my memory. Again, with the help of Wikipedia, the free encyclopedia, I want to briefly include some of that information here to show just how important and helpful Betty Crocker became to the American housewife/cook.

"Actually, Betty Crocker, is a cultural icon, a brand name and trademark of American Fortune 500 corporation General Mills. The name was first developed by the Washburn Crosby Company in 1921 as a way to give personalized response to consumer product questions. The name Betty was selected because it was viewed as a cheery, all-American name. It was paired with the last name Crocker, in honor of William Crocker, a Washburn Crosby Company director.

"Marjorie Child Husted was the creator of Betty Crocker. Ms. Husted was a home economist and business woman under whose supervision the image of Betty Crocker became that icon for General Mills. It is said that in 1945 *Fortune* magazine named Betty Crocker the second most popular American Woman; Eleanor Roosevelt was named first. Interestingly, a portrait of Betty Crocker first appeared in 1936. It subtly changed over the years, but always accommodated General Mills' cultural perception of the American homemaker as knowledgeable and caring. The current image of Betty Crocker, according to the corporation, is actually a combination of 75 real-life women of diverse backgrounds and ages. These portraits were always painted, with no real person ever having posed as a model, and they never showed the character from the shoulders down."

Since I so clearly remember the steps my mother used in her bread making, I will include here the recipe for bread that accommodated the picture of Betty Crocker. It seems to echo the process as I remember it. It is a judgment call.

White Bread
Betty Crocker method

1/2 cup warm (not hot) water	1/4 cup sugar
2 pkgs. active dry yeast	2 tablespoon salt
3 1/2 cups warm liquid (water,	1/4 cup shortening
milk, or potato water)	11 to 12 cups sifted flour

Soak yeast in 1/2 cup warm water for 5 minutes. Combine liquid with sugar and salt. Stir to dissolve. Beat in 4 cups of flour, yeast mixture, and shortening with rotary beater until smooth. Add remaining flour, mixing with a spoon until dough leaves sides of bowl. Turn out onto lightly floured board. Knead thoroughly, adding flour as necessary, until dough becomes smooth and elastic and is no longer sticky (5-10 minutes). Place in lightly greased bowl. Grease top of dough; cover with waxed paper.

Let rise in warm place until doubled (1-1 1/2 hours). Punch down and let rise again until nearly doubled. (May omit second rising to save time.)

Divide dough into equal parts; round up each portion. Shape each into loaves and place into greased loaf pans. Cover and let rise in warm place until dough reaches top of pan and corners are filled (1-1 1/2 hours) Bake in moderately hot oven (400 degrees) 45 minutes.

Superb Squash Bread

3 eggs	2 cups squash, finely grated
2 cups sugar	3 cup self-rising flour
2 teaspoons vanilla	1 tablespoon cinnamon
1 cup cooking oil	1 cup pecans (optional)

Preheat oven to 325 degrees. Blend eggs in a large bowl on medium speed until fluffy. Mix in sugar, oil, and vanilla. Slowly stir in flour and cinnamon until jut mixed. Stir in squash until evenly mixed. Pour into a well-greased 9"×13" inch baking dish or two well greased loaf pans. Bake for 45 minutes or until bread is firm and light brown. For loaf pans, add about 10 minutes to the baking time.

Cranberry Bread

1 orange, juice and rind
2 cups flour
1 cup sugar
$\frac{1}{2}$ teaspoon salt
1$\frac{1}{2}$ teaspoons baking powder
$\frac{1}{2}$ teaspoon baking soda

2 tablespoons melted shortening
1 egg
1 cup fresh cranberries,
    rough ground
1 cup chopped pecans

Preheat oven to 325 degrees. Grease and flour one 9"×5" loaf pan or two smaller loaf pans. Using a grater with small holes, grate rind off orange. Squeeze orange juice into a measuring cup and add rind and enough hot water to equal $\frac{3}{4}$ cup.

Sift flour, sugar, salt, baking powder and baking soda into a medium-size mixing bowl. Combine orange juice mixture with shortening and egg and add to dry ingredients. Mix well and stir in berries and pecans. Pour into prepared loaf pan. Bake for 45-60 minutes, until toothpick inserted in center comes out clean.

If fresh cranberries are not available, this bread can be prepared with dried cranberries that have been plumped in boiling water.

Pumpkin Apple Bread

3 cups flour
2 teaspoons cinnamon
2 teaspoons baking soda
1$\frac{1}{2}$ teaspoons salt
3 cups sugar
1 can (15 oz.) pure pumpkin

4 large eggs
1 cup vegetable oil
$\frac{1}{2}$ cup apple juice
1 large baking apple, peeled,
    cored and diced

Preheat oven to 350 degrees. Grease and flour two 9"×5" loaf pans. Combine flour, cinnamon, baking soda, and salt in large bowl. Combine sugar, pumpkin, eggs, vegetable oil and apple juice in large mixer bowl; beat until just blended. Add pumpkin mixture to flour mixture; stir just until moistened. Fold in apples and spoon batter into prepared loaf. Bake for 65-70 minutes or until wooden pick inserted in center comes out clean. Cool in pans on wire racks for 10 minutes; remove to wire rack to cool completely.

Whole Wheat Carrot Bread

2 cups milk
$^1/_4$ cup butter
1 envelope active dry yeast
$5^1/_2$ to $6^1/_2$ cups flour,
  divided use
$1^1/_2$ cup whole-wheat flour

$^1/_4$ cup firmly packed
  brown sugar
$1^1/_2$ cups cooked and mashed
  carrots (about 3 medium)
$1^1/_2$ teaspoons salt

In a 1-quart saucepan, heat milk until it just comes to a boil; stir in butter until melted. Cool to warm. In a large mixer bowl dissolve yeast in $^1/_4$ cup warm water. Add milk mixture, 2 cups flour, whole wheat flour, brown sugar, carrots and salt. Beat at medium speed, scraping bowl often, until smooth, 1-2 minutes.

By hand, stir in enough remaining flour to make dough easy to handle, not sticky. Turn dough onto lightly floured surface and knead until smooth and elastic, about 5 minutes. Place in greased bowl; turn greased side up. Cover and let rise in a warm place until it doubles, about 1 hour. Dough is ready if indentation remains when touched.

Punch down dough; divide in half. Shape each half into a loaf and place, seam side down, in two 8"×5" loaf pans. Cover; let rise until double, about 1 hour.

Heat oven to 350 degrees. Bake bread 35-45 minutes, until loaf sounds hollow when tapped. Remove from pans immediately and brush tops with butter.

Whole wheat carrot bread—just the name itself sounds good for you!

Carrot Bread
(No yeast needed)

1 1/2 cups flour
1 teaspoon baking soda
2 teaspoons baking powder
1 teaspoon cinnamon
1/2 teaspoon salt
1 cup vegetable oil
1 cup packed brown sugar

3 eggs
1/2 cup chopped pecans
1/2 cup canned, diced pineapple, drained
1/2 cup raisins
1 cup finely shredded raw carrots

Heat oven to 350 degrees. Grease and flour a 9" loaf pan. Sift flour, baking soda, baking powder, cinnamon, and salt into a mixing bowl. In a separate bowl, whisk together oil, sugar, and eggs. Stir the liquid mixture into the flour mixture; mix well. Add pecans, pineapple, raisins, and carrots; stir again. Fill the pan two-thirds full with batter. Bake for about 20-30 minutes.

Friendship Bread

1 cup vegetable oil
1 1/2 cups sugar
1 teaspoon vanilla
3 large eggs
1/2 teaspoon salt
2 teaspoons cinnamon
2 1/2 cups flour

1 1/4 cups milk
1/2 teaspoon baking soda
1 box (3.4 oz.) instant vanilla pudding
1 1/2 teaspoon baking powder
1/3 cup chopped pecans (optional)

Preheat oven to 325 degrees. Combine oil, sugar, vanilla, eggs, salt, and cinnamon in a large bowl. Add flour, milk, soda, pudding mix, baking powder, and pecans. Mix well. Grease two large loaf pans and sprinkle with a mixture of sugar and cinnamon. Pour in bread mixture and sprinkle with sugar and cinnamon on top. Bake for one hour. Good with drizzled icing over top.

> "Good bread is the most fundamentally satisfying of all foods; and good bread with fresh butter, the greatest of feasts."
> —JAMES BEARD (1903-1985)

Lemon-Poppy Seed Bread

3 cups flour	2 cups sugar
2 teaspoon baking powder	1 cup vegetable oil
$1/4$ teaspoon salt	$3/4$ cup milk
2 tablespoons poppy seeds	1 teaspoon vanilla
2 tablespoons coarsely	$1/2$ teaspoon almond extract
grated lemon rind	3 large eggs

Preheat oven to 350 degrees. Grease bottoms only of two 9" × 5" loaf pans. Combine first 5 ingredients (flour through lemon rind) in a large bowl and blend well. Combine sugar and next 5 ingredients (sugar through eggs) in a mixing bowl; beat with a mixer at medium speed until well blended. Add wet mixture to dry mixture, stirring just until dry ingredients are moistened. Pour batter into prepared pans. Bake 1 hour or until a wooden pick inserted in center comes out clean.

Prepare glaze: Combine 2 cups powdered sugar (sifted), 2 teaspoons coarsely grated lemon rind, and $1/4$ cup lemon juice. Remove loaves from pans and pour glaze over warm bread.

Banana Bread

$3^1/2$ cups sifted flour	$3/4$ cup shortening
1 tablespoons baking powder	$1^1/2$ cups sugar
1 teaspoon salt	3 eggs
1 teaspoon baking soda	1 teaspoon vanilla
2 cups mashed ripe bananas	$3/4$ cup milk
2 tablespoons lemon juice	$3/4$ cup chopped pecans

Preheat oven to 350 degrees. Sift together flour, baking powder, salt, and baking soda. Combine banana and lemon juice; mix well. With an electric mixer at medium speed, cream the shortening and sugar in a bowl until fluffy. Add eggs and vanilla, and beat thoroughly until very light and fluffy. Add the dry ingredients alternately with the milk; fold in the banana mixture and nuts. Beat after each addition. Pour into two greased 8"×4"×2" loaf pans. Bake one hour or until a cake tester comes out clean. Cool in pans for 10 minutes. Remove from pans and cool on racks. Wrap in foil or plastic wrap and let stand in cool place overnight before slicing or freezing.

Bettye's Best Banana Bread

1³/₄ cup flour
¹/₄ teaspoon salt
1 teaspoon baking soda
1¹/₂ sticks butter, softened
1¹/₂ cups sugar
2 eggs

¹/₄ cup buttermilk
1 teaspoon vanilla
¹/₂ to 1 cup chopped pecans
1 cup well-mashed
overripe bananas

Preheat over to 350 degrees. Grease and flour two 8"×4" loaf pans. Combine flour, salt, and baking soda. Cream together butter and sugar until light and fluffy. Add eggs, one at a time, beating well after each addition. Add flour mixture and buttermilk alternately. Beat batter for 2-3 minutes. Stir in vanilla, nuts, and bananas. Spoon into loaf pans. Bake about 50 minutes or until a toothpick inserted in center comes out clean. Cool before adding the following glaze: Stir together 1 cup powdered sugar and 2-3 tablespoons lemon juice until smooth. Pour over cooled banana bread.

Absolute Best Banana Nut Bread

1 cup butter
1 cup white sugar
1 cup brown sugar
4 eggs
¹/₄ teaspoon salt
2 teaspoons baking soda

2 cups all-purpose flour
1 cup wheat flour
1 cup wheat germ
6 large ripe bananas, mashed
1 cup chopped pecans

Preheat over to 250 degrees. Cream butter and both sugars. Add eggs. Sift together salt, baking soda, and flours. Add wheat germ to flour mixture. Alternately add flour mixture and mashed bananas to the creamed mixture. Add pecans to batter. Pour into two well greased loaf pans. Sprinkle with a little brown sugar, wheat germ, and a few chopped pecans. Bake for 1-2 hours or until a toothpick inserted into center comes out clean.

```
"Dinner is ready when the smoke alarm goes off!"
                    —ANONYMOUS
```

Coffee Can Bread *by Amber Boerner*

4 cups unsifted flour
1 package dry yeast
$^1/_2$ cup water
$^1/_2$ cup butter

$^1/_4$ cup sugar
2 beaten eggs
2 (1-pound size) coffee
    cans with lids

Mix flour with yeast, set aside. Combine water, milk, butter, sugar, and beaten eggs in a saucepan. Cook over low heat until butter melts. Cool five minutes. Add flour/yeast mixture. Knead on floured surface just until dough is smooth. Coat inside coffee cans with cooking spray. Divide dough into two balls. Place one in each can, cover with lid. Let rise until 1 inch from lid. Remove lids and bake in 375 degree oven for 35 minutes.

Cornbread

3 cups buttermilk
$^1/_2$ cup vegetable oil
2 large eggs
2 cups flour
2 cups cornmeal

1 cup sugar
2 tablespoons baking powder
2 teaspoons baking soda
2 teaspoons salt

Heat oven to 325 degrees. Butter a 9"×13" baking pan. Combine buttermilk, oil, and eggs in a bowl and whisk to combine well. In a large bowl stir together flour, cornmeal, sugar, baking powder, baking soda, and salt. Pour the liquid ingredients into the dry ingredients and whisk together until combined. Pour the batter into the prepared pan and place on middle rack in the oven. Bake for 45 minutes, or up to 1 hour until the top is golden brown and a toothpick inserted into the middle comes out clean. 15-18 servings.

**Skillet-made cornbread—
with beans, stew, chili.
It goes great with
practically everything!**

Blueberry Muffins

2 cups flour
1 cup sugar
2 teaspoons baking powder
$^1/_2$ teaspoon baking soda
$^3/_4$ teaspoon salt

2 eggs
1 cup sour cream
$^1/_2$ cup milk
$^1/_4$ cup butter, melted
2 cups blueberries

Heat oven to 400 degrees. Mix flour, sugar, baking powder, baking soda, and salt. Set aside. Beat eggs; add sour cream, milk and butter to eggs. Add flour mixture to egg mixture. Add blueberries; fold in gently. Divide batter among 18 paper lined muffin cups. Bake until done, about 20 minutes.

Magic Muffins

Placed in a tightly covered container, this batter will keep for four weeks and improves over time. Do not stir at any time after refrigerating or when preparing to bake muffins. Makes enough for four dozen muffins.

1 box (14 oz.) Raisin Bran
5 cups flour
3 cups sugar
5 teaspoons baking soda
2 teaspoons salt

4 cups buttermilk
1 cup vegetable oil
4 eggs, beaten
1$^1/_2$ cup dried, sweetened
  cranberries

Combine cereal, flour, sugar, baking soda, and salt in a large bowl, mix well. Combine buttermilk, oil and eggs in a separate bowl and whisk well. Pour egg mixture into cereal mixture; stir until just blended. Fold in cranberries.

Preheat oven to 400 degrees. Grease as many muffin cups as wanted. Spoon batter into prepared pan. Bake 18 minutes, or until a toothpick comes out clean. Cool in muffin tin for 10 minutes. Serve warm or remove to wire rack to cool. (Place remainder of batter in refrigerator. See above note.)

"Many people have eaten my cooking and gone on to lead normal lives."

—ANONYMOUS

Bran Muffins

2 cups boiling water	5½ cups flour, sifted
2 cups raisins	1 cup chopped nuts
5 teaspoons baking soda	4 cups All Bran cereal
1 cup butter (2 sticks)	2 cups 40% Bran Flakes
2 cups sugar	4 eggs, beaten
1 quart buttermilk	1 teaspoon salt

Combine first three ingredients in a bowl and set aside. In a large bowl cream sugar and butter. Combine beaten eggs with buttermilk in a separate container. Mix together flour, cereals, salt, and nuts in another bowl. Alternately add dry and wet ingredients to creamed mixture until just moistened. Stir in raisin mixture last. Store batter in refrigerator until you want to bake fresh muffins. The batter will last for 6 weeks. When ready to bake, fill greased muffin tins ¾ full and bake at 375 degrees 20-25 minutes. Yields 4 dozen muffins.

Dream Coffee Cake

1 pkg. (18 oz.) yellow cake mix	1 cup sour cream
1 cup vegetable oil	¾ cup sugar
4 eggs	1½ teaspoon cinnamon
	1¾ cup pecans, chopped

Preheat oven to 350 degrees. Grease a 9"×13" pan. Combine cake mix, vegetable oil, eggs, and sour cream in a large bowl. Beat two minutes with mixer at low speed, scraping sides frequently. Mix sugar, cinnamon, and pecans in a separate medium bowl. Spread half of the batter in pan. Sprinkle half of the pecan mixture over the top. Repeat with remaining batter and pecan mixture. Bake 40 minutes or until wooden toothpick inserted in middle comes out clean. Serves 20.

Smell that cinnamon!

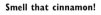

Banana Coffee Cake

1 (8 oz.) package cream cheese, softened	1 cup mashed, ripe banana
	1 teaspoon vanilla
¹/₂ cup butter, softened	2¹/₄ cups flour
1¹/₂ cups sugar	1¹/₂ teaspoons baking powder
2 eggs	¹/₂ teaspoon baking soda

In a mixing bowl, beat cream cheese, butter, and sugar. Add the eggs, one at a time, beating well after each addition. Add the banana and the vanilla. In a separate bowl, combine flour, baking powder, and baking soda, gradually adding to the creamed mixture; set aside.

TOPPING:

1 cup chopped pecans	1 teaspoon cinnamon
2 tablespoons sugar	

Combine pecans, sugar, and cinnamon in another bowl; add half to the creamed batter. Pour into a greased 9"×13"×2" baking pan. Sprinkle with the remaining topping. Bake at 350 degrees for 25-30 minutes until toothpick inserted into center comes out clean. Cool on a wire rack. 12 servings.

Momma's Doughnuts *by Clara E. Hahn*

1 cup milk	2 eggs, beaten
¹/₄ to ¹/₂ yeast cake	¹/₄ teaspoon nutmeg
¹/₄ cup warm water	¹/₃ cup butter or other lard
1 teaspoon salt	Flour to make dough
1 cup sugar	

Scald and cool milk. Mix yeast with water and add to milk. Add a little of the sugar. Allow this to rise to double in bulk. Add melted butter, salt, sugar, eggs, and beat until well beaten. Mix nutmeg with flour enough to make a stiff dough. Knead on floured board and roll dough to ¹/₄ inch thick. Cut with doughnut cutter. Allow to stand on board 1 hour. Fry in deep fat. Drain when browned. Roll in sugar or frost with icing.

Antique doughnut cutter with sticker still attached which says "Dooley's" of Fredericksburg.

Momma's Quick Buttermilk Rolls
by Clara E. Hahn

$^1/_2$ cup buttermilk, scalded
2 cakes yeast
$^1/_4$ cup warm water
$^1/_4$ cup sugar

$^1/_2$ cup melted shortening
1 teaspoon salt
$^1/_2$ teaspoon soda
$4^1/_2$ cups flour

Scald buttermilk in double boiler. Dissolve yeast in warm water. Add buttermilk and cool to lukewarm. Add sugar, shortening and salt; then the flour and soda which have been sifted together. Mix well and let stand 10 minutes. Roll out and cut or shape as desired. Allow to rise until double in bulk about 30 minutes. Bake in a hot oven 425 degrees for 10-12 minutes. Makes 24 rolls.

No-Knead Refrigerator Rolls

$^2/_3$ cup canola oil
1 tablespoon salt
2 cups warm water
2 pkgs. dry yeast (dissolve in
$^1/_4$ cup warm water)

$^1/_4$ cup sugar
$^1/_2$ cup wheat germ
2 eggs
6 cups flour

Mix oil, salt, water, yeast, sugar, wheat germ, and eggs in a large bowl. Add flour, 1 cup at a time, stirring after each addition. Cover with a plastic wrap, and place in refrigerator for at least 2 hours before using. This dough lasts up to five days in the refrigerator. To bake, make 2-inch balls from the dough. Place them in a large greased cake pan, about 1 inch apart, and cover with a damp cloth until they double in size. Preheat oven to 375 degrees. Bake for about 20 minutes or until golden. Invert pan to remove rolls. Serve warm.

> Originally, buttermilk was the lowfat liquid remaining after churning cream into butter.
> Today buttermilk is made by adding lactic acid-producing bacteria to pasteurized or ultrapasteurized milk with nonfat dry milk solids. The product is heated until the desired acidity is achieved, then cooled to stop fermentation.
> Today, depending on the level of milk fat in the product, buttermilk may be called cultured, lowfat, or skim buttermilk.

Pineapple Bread Casserole

3 cups cubed white bread
1/2 cup butter, melted
4 eggs

1/2 cup sugar
1 can (20 oz.) crushed
    pineapple, undrained

Preheat oven to 350 degrees. Butter a baking dish. Toss bread and butter together. In separate small bowl, beat together eggs, sugar, and pineapple with juice. Combine pineapple mixture with bread mixture; put in prepared baking dish. Bake uncovered until set and browned, about 20-25 minutes. Makes 6 servings.

Café Brulot Bread Pudding

1 1/2 milk
1/2 stick butter
2/3 cup sugar
4 cups day old bread crumbs
1/2 cup raisins
1 cup chopped apples

3 eggs, beaten
1/8 teaspoon salt
1/2 teaspoon nutmeg
1 teaspoon vanilla
2 tablespoons lemon juice
1 tablespoon cinnamon

Preheat oven to 350 degrees. Scald milk. Melt butter in milk and stir in sugar. Place bread, raisins, and apples in a 9"×13" greased baking dish. Pour milk mixture over bread. Stir and let stand. Beat eggs with salt, nutmeg, vanilla, and lemon juice. Stir into bread mixture. Sprinkle with cinnamon. Bake 35 to 40 minutes. Serve warm with lemon sauce.

SAUCE:
1/2 cup sugar
1 tablespoon cornstarch
1 cup water
2 tablespoons butter

1/2 tablespoon lemon juice
1/4 teaspoon lemon extract
Dash of salt

Combine sugar and cornstarch in saucepan. Stir in water and heat over medium heat. Cook, stirring constantly until it thickens. Add butter, lemon juice, lemon extract, and salt. Cook 1 minute more and serve warm over bread pudding.

CHAPTER NINE

Soups and Chowders

In the 1939 farm kitchen and thinking about soup as it pertained to my young kitchen years, it seems to me that soup was something we cooked mostly during the summer months as opposed to normal soups usually served in winter. This is because during the summer months we belonged to a butcher club and when we were down to the bone of our cut of beef, we boiled the bones to be sure to get all the meat. The boiled meat was then trimmed of fat and usually ground up to become either sandwich filling or it was used in a hash along with potatoes and onions. The water the bones were boiled in became stock for vegetable soup.

To the modern cook today that may seem drastic but remember we were in a depression. When that melancholy era was just beginning, people all over the United States were in a terrible funk. Compared to city folk, people on farms had the best possible living circumstance. We could raise our own food. But, farmers and ranchers nevertheless were deeply involved, not by their choosing, but because of an event in our history when the U.S. Department of Agriculture conceived of an unbelievable action that directed that federal agents should go out to farms and ranches and shoot all the cows, calves, and even some sheep and goats that they deemed "surplus" livestock. And, as if that was not harsh enough, the farmers and ranchers were not allowed to save or cook the meat. Everything had to be burned or buried. My father talked about this and I will never forget how his face registered pain and I can still hear him, ". . . how it hurt to see blood running through the cow pen when they shot some of my livestock."

I understand this happened around 1929 (I was born in 1932). My father went on to explain that the Supreme Court of the United States finally declared the whole thing unconstitutional in 1936. As with my parents, this experience left a lasting impression on generations and instilled the value that we must not ever waste or throw away food—any food. It became deeply ingrained in my mind and it still makes sense again today. I cringe when I see waste. In absolute truth, we realize that sometimes we either irritate or amuse youth with our frugality. Instead, perhaps you should give serious thought to understanding and forgiving my generation. Hopefully our nation and you will never again sink to a similar depression situation of the 1930s.

Returning to the subject of soup: Momma and I only cooked vegetable/beef soup. Today, however, my sixty year recipe collection reflects several soup recipes. I hope you will enjoy them.

Taco Soup

My son Roger and daughter-in-law Pam Durden, served this with cornbread to a mob of fans prior to a regional football play-off game in an Austin stadium near their home. Two of my grandsons, Jesse and Josh Durden, were important members of the Bobcat team.

This recipe is from the 80th anniversary edition cookbook produced by the St. Peter's Evangelical Lutheran Church, Elgin, Texas, in 1998.

1 1/2 lbs. hamburger	1 can whole kernel corn
1 onion, chopped	1 can Ro-Tel tomatoes
1 can kidney beans	1 can diced tomatoes
1 can pinto beans	1 pkg. Taco Mix
1 can black beans	1 pkg. ranch salad dressing (dry)

Brown meat. Add onion. Drain off fat. Place all ingredients in a Dutch oven. Heat at least until heated throughout.

"Food is our common ground, a universal experience."
—JAMES BEARD (1903-1985)

No-Fuss Potato Soup

Robin and George Hale served this to one of our Soup and Bread suppers before Lenten services. Sometimes the most uncomplicated recipes are the best all around.

6 cups peeled, diced potatoes
5 cups water
2 cups diced onions
1/2 cup diced celery
1/2 cup chopped carrots
1/4 cup butter
4 teaspoons chicken
    bouillon granules

2 teaspoons salt
1/4 teaspoon pepper
1 can (12 oz.) evaporated milk
3 tablespoons chopped
    fresh parsley
Cheddar cheese (8 oz.)
    shredded, sharp

Combine all ingredients except milk, parsley, and cheese in slow cooker or soup pot. Cover and cook until vegetables are tender. Stir in milk and parsley. Stir in cheese until it melts. Heat thoroughly.

For added flavor, stir in 3 slices bacon, browned until crisp and crumbled. Top individual servings with chopped chives.

Potato Bacon Chowder

2 cups peeled, cubed potatoes
1 cup water
8 bacon strips
1 cup chopped onion
1/2 cup chopped celery
1 can (10 3/4 oz.) condensed
    cream of chicken soup,
    undiluted

1 3/4 cups milk
1 cup (9 oz.) sour cream
1/2 teaspoon salt
Dash of pepper
1 tablespoon minced
    fresh parsley

In a large saucepan, cover and cook potatoes in 1 cup water until tender. Meanwhile, cook bacon in a skillet until crisp; remove to a paper towel to drain. In the same skillet, sauté onion and celery in drippings until tender; drain. Add to undrained potatoes. Stir in soup, milk, sour cream, salt, and pepper. Cook over low heat for 10 minutes or until heated through. (*Do not boil.*) Crumble bacon; set aside 1/4 cup. Add remaining bacon to soup along with parsley. Sprinkle with reserved bacon. Serves 6.

French Onion Soup

Maintain the rich flavor of this classic soup by stir-frying the onions in dry sherry and adding a dash of Worcestershire sauce. No need for lots of cheese, simply sprinkle a small amount of grated Parmesan over a piping hot bowl of soup and enjoy!

2 medium onions, thinly sliced
4 tablespoon dry sherry
4 cups fat-free beef broth
1 teaspoon Worcestershire

4 slices (1 oz.) French bread
2 tablespoons Parmesan
   cheese, grated

In a large saucepan, combine the onions and sherry and sauté for about 6 minutes or until onions are tender. Add beef broth and Worcestershire. Bring to a boil, then reduce heat and cover and simmer for 10 minutes. Meanwhile, toast French bread until golden brown. Place one piece of toast into each serving bowl, then pour on the soup. Sprinkle $1/2$ tablespoon grated cheese on top of each serving.

Beef Soup

$1^1/2$ pounds lean ground beef
1 garlic clove, minced
1 large onion, chopped
1 quart vegetable juice
1 tablespoon brown sugar
1 bay leaf

2 cans ($10^3/4$ oz.) cream of
   celery soup (do not dilute)
2 cups thinly sliced carrots
1 cup thinly sliced celery
Salt and pepper to taste

Pan fry ground beef, garlic, and onion together. Drain and put in large soup pot. Add juice, sugar, bay leaf, and soup. Microwave carrots and celery until tender and add to soup mixture. Simmer for $1/2$ hour or longer. Add salt and pepper. Serves 6-8.

> "Good soup is one of the prime ingredients of good living. For soup can do more to lift the spirits and stimulate the appetite than any other one dish."
>
> —LOUIS P. DE GOUY, *The Soup Book* (1949)

Sante Fe Soup *by Una Kunkel*

Thanks to Violet Alexander and the Travis County Homemakers and their simply delicious recipe book presented to me after a speaking engagement to that group in Austin. Wonderful book— jam packed with recipes such as this one.

1 lb. ground meat	1 can stewed tomatoes
1 onion, chopped	1 can Rotel tomatoes
1 can whole kernel corn	1 lb. Velveeta cheese
1 can Ranch style beans	

Cook ground meat and onion; drain. Put in crockpot. Add corn, beans, and both cans of tomatoes; heat. Add Velveeta cheese and continue cooking until melted. Serve over tortilla chips.

Ham 'N Cheese Chowder *by Faye Davis*
(Travis County Homemakers Cookbook)

1 cup water	3 tablespoons flour
Dash of salt	Dash of pepper
2 cups peeled and	3 cups milk
cubed potatoes	1$^1/_2$ cups cooked ham, diced
3 tablespoons butter	$^1/_2$ cup (6 oz.) grated
$^3/_4$ cup chopped onion	cheddar cheese

Bring water to boil; add salt and potatoes and reduce heat. Cook 15 minutes or until potatoes are tender. Drain, reserving liquid. Set potatoes aside. Add enough water to reserved liquid to make 1 cup. Set aside.

Melt butter in 3 quart pan. Add onion and sauté until tender. Blend in flour and pepper. Stir in milk and potato liquid. Cook over medium heat until bubbly and slightly thickened. Add potatoes and ham and heat gently. Remove from heat and stir in cheese. Top with croutons if desired.

CHAPTER TEN

Breakfast Specials

Tomato, Pepper, Bread and Ricotta Frittata

12 large eggs
$^1/_3$ cup heavy cream
1$^1/_3$ cups cubed (1 inch) day-old bread
3 tablespoons extra virgin olive oil, divided use
1 onion, cut into $^1/_2$ inch thick strips

1 each red and green bell peppers, cut into $^1/_4$ inch strips
$^1/_2$ cup ripe cherry tomatoes, cut in half
1 tablespoon unsalted butter
$^1/_2$ cup fresh ricotta

Preheat oven to 350 degrees. In a large bowl, beat eggs, heavy cream, and salt and pepper to taste. Add bread cubes; let soak until softened, about 15 minutes. Set aside.

Heat 2 tablespoons olive oil in a 10-inch skillet over medium heat. Add onion, cook until wilted. Add peppers, stirring until crisp-tender. Season with salt and pepper. Stir in tomatoes. Add butter and remaining oil to skillet. Heat until foaming. Now pour egg and bread mixture into pan; cook over medium heat without stirring.

Meanwhile add ricotta by tablespoonfuls, forming little pockets on top. Continue cooking until bottom is lightly browned, about 5 minutes. There should be a few bubbles around edges.

Once bottom crust has formed, transfer skillet to preheated oven, cook until center is firm to touch about 15-20 minutes. To serve hot, let frittata stand at room temperature about 15 minutes.

Southwest Oven Omelet

1 can (4.5 oz.) green chilies
2 jars (3.9 oz.) mushrooms
Monterey Jack cheese (16 oz.),
   grated

1 pound diced ham
1 can (12-oz.) evaporated milk
8 eggs
2 tablespoons flour

Preheat oven to 300 degrees. Generously butter a 9"×13" baking dish. In a medium sized bowl, mix together chilies, mushrooms, cheese, and ham. Spoon the mixture evenly over the bottom of baking dish. In the same bowl, whisk together evaporated milk, eggs, and flour. Pour this over the cheese mixture and bake for 1 hour. Serves 6-8. Serve with fresh fruit and corn muffins.

Basic French Toast

2 tablespoons (¼ stick
   unsalted butter) divided use)
8 slices (⅛ inch thick) good
   quality bread (divided use)
1 large egg

1 large egg yolk
2 tablespoons sugar
1 teaspoon vanilla
1½ cups half-and-half

In a medium bowl, whisk together egg, egg yolk, sugar, and vanilla until pale and foamy. Stir in half-and-half, mixing until smooth. Warm half the butter in a large non-stick skillet. Dip 4 slices bread in egg mixture, coating both sides. Once butter is foamy, add slices to pan and brown lightly for 2-3 minutes on each side. Remove from heat, keep warm and repeat using the remaining butter, bread, and batter. Serve warm, garnished with fresh fruit, and serve with maple syrup.

A favorite of just about every child is french toast topped with fresh fruit.

Overnight Breakfast Bars

1¼ cups flour	1 cup sugar
1½ cups old-fashioned oats	½ cup packed brown sugar
2 tablespoons Uncle Sam	⅔ cup butter, softened
Cereal (optional)	2 eggs
1 teaspoon baking power	1⅓ cups buttermilk or
1 tablespoon baking soda	plain yogurt
¼ teaspoon salt	2 medium apples, peeled,
2 teaspoons cinnamon	cored, and chopped

Grease 9"×13" baking dish. Combine flour, oats, cereal, baking powder, baking soda, salt, and cinnamon in a medium bowl; set aside.

Combine granulated sugar, brown sugar, and butter in a large bowl. Beat with a mixer at low speed until just blended. Increase speed to high and beat well. Blend in eggs and buttermilk. Decrease speed to low and gradually add flour mixture, beating until just blended and scraping sides of bowl. Fold in apples. Pour into pan.

TOPPING:

1 cup pecans, broken	1 teaspoon cinnamon
½ cup packed brown sugar	

To prepare topping, combine pecans, brown sugar, and cinnamon; mix well. Sprinkle evenly over batter. Cover with plastic wrap and refrigerate overnight.

Next morning, preheat oven to 350 degrees. Uncover pan and let stand for 30 minutes. Bake 45 minutes or until toothpick inserted in the center comes out clean. Serve warm. Serves 18.

"'When you wake up in the morning, Pooh,' said Piglet at last, 'what's the first thing you say to yourself?'
'What's for breakfast?' said Pooh.
'What do you say, Piglet?' 'I say.
"I wonder what's going to happen exciting today?' said Piglet.
Pooh nodded thoughtfully. 'It's the same thing,' he said."

—A. A. MILNE, *The House at Pooh Corner*

Simple Quick Breakfast Casserole

8 eggs
6 slices bread, cubed small
1 lb. sausage, browned
   and crumbled

2 cups milk
1 cup sharp cheddar cheese,
   grated
1 teaspoon salt

Mix all the above ingredients together and pour into a 9"×13" greased baking dish. Refrigerate overnight. Bake at 350 degrees for about 45 minutes.

Lemon Cranberry Loaves

1¼ cups finely chopped
   cranberries (fresh)
½ cup finely chopped pecans
¼ cup sugar
1 box Lemon Supreme cake mix

¾ cup milk
2 oz. cream cheese, room
   temperature, cut into pieces
4 large eggs
Powdered sugar

Grease and flour two 8½" x 4½" loaf pans. Heat oven to 350 degrees. Stir together cranberries, pecans, and sugar in large bowl, set aside.

Combine dry cake mix, milk, and cream cheese in a large bowl. Beat at medium speed with mixer for 3 minutes. Add eggs, 1 at a time, beating for 2 minutes. Fold in cranberry mixture. Divide between the two prepared pans. Bake 45-50 minutes or until toothpick inserted in centers comes out clean. Cool in pans for 15 minutes. Loosen loaves and invert onto cooling rack. Cool. Dust with powdered sugar. Serve with butter and jam. Freezes really well.

Coffee and a slice of Lemon Cranberry Loaf—what a way to start the day!

Large Cinnamon Roll *by Monica Wallace*

This is the most often requested food for a Durden Family Gathering. Our good family friend, Monica Wallace gave me this recipe. Once again, it is another heritage recipe. Monica got this recipe from her mom, Eugenie Dupuy Madden—who got it from her mother, Emily Ledet Dupuy.

1 cup boiling water	1 cup warm milk
$^3/_4$ cup sugar	2 pkg. active dry yeast
1 cup shortening	2 eggs
1$^1/_2$ teaspoons salt	6-7 cups bread flour

Mix first four ingredients in a large mixing bowl. Make sure the sugar dissolves and cool to lukewarm. In a separate small mixing bowl, dissolve the yeast in the warm milk.

Beat the eggs and combine them with the first four ingredients. Add the yeast mixture. Add 3 cups of bread flour and beat in by hand only. Continue to add flour, one cup at a time.

Knead dough and let rise until double in size. Spread dough on a lightly floured surface and roll out into a oval shape about $^1/_2$" thick. Spread butter over the dough. Sprinkle sugar and cinnamon over the butter.

From the closest edge to you, start to roll the dough until you have rolled the entire oval. With a sharp knife, cut small openings down the role. Spread butter on top of the roll. Place the roll in a half moon shape on a cookie sheet. Bake in a preheated oven at 400 degrees for 30 minutes or until golden brown.

After the roll cools, mix powdered sugar, butter and half and half with 1 teaspoon vanilla. Pour icing over the roll and allow icing to cover the roll.

Cinnamon was one of the first known spices. The Romans believed cinnamon's fragrance sacred and burned it at funerals. It was used in ancient Egypt 5,000 years ago and is mentioned numerous time in the Old Testament of the Bible.

Banana Breakfast Coffee Cake

2 cups flour	$^2/_3$ cup sugar
1 teaspoon baking soda	2 eggs
1 teaspoon baking powder	1 teaspoon vanilla
$^1/_2$ teaspoon nutmeg	1 cup very ripe mashed banana
$^1/_2$ teaspoon salt	$^1/_3$ cup milk
$^1/_2$ cup butter, softened	

Preheat oven 350 degrees. Coat a 9" baking pan with cooking spray. Prepare topping.

Combine flour, baking soda, baking powder, nutmeg, and salt in a medium bowl. Beat butter with a mixer at medium speed about 30 seconds or until smooth. Gradually add sugar and beat three to four minutes until fluffy. Add eggs, one at a time, beating well after each. Add vanilla and bananas and beat until well blended. Add the flour mixture alternately with milk, mixing after each addition only until smooth. Pour batter into prepared pan and sprinkle with topping. Bake about 35 minutes until toothpick inserted into center comes out clean. Cool in pan on wire rack. Serves warm or at room temperature. 10 servings.

TOPPING:

$^1/_2$ cup flour	6 tablespoons cold
$^1/_2$ cup firmly packed	unsalted butter
light brown sugar	$^1/_2$ cup finely chopped pecans
1 teaspoon cinnamon	

Combine flour, brown sugar, cinnamon, and butter in a food processor until mixture resembles fine crumbs. Stir in pecans. Set aside.

Donald Durden, the oldest son born to the Jerry Durden Jr. Family.

CHAPTER ELEVEN

Classic Collectors' Recipes

Light and Easy Avocado Dip

2 avocados, lightly mashed
1/4 teaspoon salt
1 tablespoon lemon juice
1/2 teaspoon Worcestershire

1 medium tomato, peeled,
   seeded and chopped fine
A dash or two of hot sauce,
   to taste

Combine all ingredients and serve with corn or tortilla chips.

Po Po Restaurant's House Dressing

1 cup sugar
1 cup Wesson Oil
1/2 cup vinegar
2/3 cup catsup

1 tablespoon Worcestershire
Salt, pepper, to taste
Garlic, peeled and leave whole

Place whole garlic in a jar along with the other ingredients. Shake well and often. Best after a week in refrigerator.

Bernice Schaetter's Dip

Cream cheese (8 oz.), softened
2 tablespoons French dressing
1 tablespoon onion, finely grated

1/3 teaspoon salt
1/3 cup catsup

Mix all ingredients and refrigerate overnight before serving. Super!

Marinade Special *by Jasanda Watson*

$^1/_2$ cup oil	1 tablespoon pepper
$^3/_4$ cup soy sauce	$^1/_2$ cup red wine vinegar
$^1/_4$ cup water	$^1/_3$ cup lemon juice
2 tablespoons dry mustard	2-3 cloves garlic, pressed
1$^1/_2$ teaspoons salt	

Marinade at room temperature 4-5 hours. Grill meat. Reserve marinade in pan and slow boil 4-5 minutes. Use for sauce when serving.

Uncle Emil's (Lange) Bar-B-Q Sauce

1 pound butter	8 teaspoons prepared mustard
1 cup vinegar	3-4 teaspoons chili powder
1 cup water	2 teaspoons sugar
2 cups catsup	4-6 tablespoons Worcestershire

Add all ingredients to saucepan and bring to boil. Simmer 10 minutes. When bar-b-q is almost done (last 15 to 20) minutes, over medium to warm coals only, brush bar-b-q sauce generously all over the meat. Turn often after sauce has been applied and watch that it does not burn. (It will burn easily if fire is too hot.) This recipe will sauce 15 pounds of meat.

Cheese Ball

2 pkg. (8 oz.) cream cheese	2 teaspoons Worcestershire
1 pound sharp cheddar cheese	Paprika
$^1/_2$ cup green onions, chopped	1 small can deviled ham
2 teaspoons pimiento, chopped	or chicken
1 teaspoon spicy brown mustard	Pecans, chopped
1 teaspoon lemon juice	

Mix all ingredients together and shape into a ball. Chill. Roll in chopped pecans.

Spinach Balls

The recipe below is from Sylvia Lindner-Vogt and was an immediate addition to my collection. It is one of the best tasting appetizers I've ever tasted. Great party offering.

2 pkgs. (10-oz.) frozen chopped spinach	$3/4$ cup melted butter
3 cups herbed-seasoned stuffing mix	$1/2$ cup grated Parmesan cheese
1 large onion, chopped finely	$1\,1/2$ teaspoon black pepper
6 eggs, well beaten	$1\,1/2$ garlic salt
	$1/2$ teaspoon thyme

Cook spinach according to directions. Drain well and squeeze to remove excess moisture. Combine spinach and remaining ingredients, mixing well. Shape mixture in $3/4$" balls and place on lightly greased cookie sheets. Bake for 15-20 minutes at 325 degrees. Makes 11 dozen balls. (These can easily be frozen unbaked and used as needed. Freeze on cookie sheets and then store in plastic bags.)

The Scent of Christmas

When we have finished baking for Christmas, there is a sense of excitement. We cook a batch of the Scent of Christmas to permeate the house throughout. This recipe will give your home that very special scent that we all remember so well.

16 oz. apple juice	1 cup water
23 oz. pineapple juice	1 stick cinnamon
1 cup water	$1/2$ tablespoon whole allspice
16 oz. apple juice	$1/2$ tablespoon ground ginger
23 oz. pineapple juice	

Mix together all ingredients, put in a saucepan and simmer. Add water or more juice from time to time when the mixture cooks down or becomes too thick.

Store in a covered plastic container and keep in freezer or refrigerator when not in use. This lasts and lasts and makes your house smell wonderful for the holidays.

Cheese Straws *by Ann (Wilson) Goforth*

Recipe found in the Cooking in Comfort *recipe book published by members of Comfort Historical Society in 1961.*

³/₄ pound sharp cheese
1 cup flour
¹/₂ teaspoon salt
1 tablespoon cream

¹/₄ cup butter, melted
4 drops Tabasco sauce
¹/₄ teaspoon Paprika

Grate cheese; mix in order given. Use hands to mix if necessary, as dough is very stiff. Roll on floured pastry cloth and cut into strips. This breaks easily—patch and put together. Bake at 350 degrees for 10 minutes.

Seven Layer Dip
From Feeding the Flock, *Liberal, Kansas*

1 pkg. (16 oz.) sour cream
1 pkg. Taco seasoning
2 cans (16 oz.) refried beans
1 jar (16 oz.) salsa
2 cups shredded sharp
   cheddar cheese

1 can (4 oz.) black olives,
   sliced
2 cups shredded lettuce
1 large tomato, chopped
2 avocados, diced
¹/₂ cup green onion, chopped

Mix sour cream and taco seasoning. Chill for 30 minutes. Combine beans and salsa in saucepan and heat on medium until evenly blended. Let cool. Spread beans and salsa in 11"×13" pan. Spread sour cream/taco seasoning mixture over beans. Layer cheese, olives, lettuce, tomatoes, avocados, and green onions. Serve with tortilla chips.

Consuming cheese immediately after meals or as a between-meal snack helps to reduce the risk of tooth decay. Certain cheeses—aged Cheddar, Swiss, blue, Monterey Jack, Brie, Gouda and processed American cheese—have been shown to help prevent tooth decay. Calcium, phosphorus and other components in cheese may contribute to this beneficial effect.

CHAPTER TWELVE

Wrapping It Up—Literally
Bill and Mae Go Phyllo

One of the fun, new experiences for me in my fourteen years of marriage to Bill Nelson is to have a person in the kitchen with me— standing at ready to do whatever he can to help in any cooking process. Like washing the used mixing bowls and stuff even while I'm cooking. Alternatively, he also peels whatever is the fruit or veggie of the current cooking venture or breaking pecans, etc. For me at least, having four hands and two brains, and fun conversation going on in the kitchen is both wonderful and super great. All of which made for this hilarious story. I want to incorporate it into this book, my latest writing challenge: a combination history/ cookbook, of sorts!

This story begins in that we're both always on the lookout for new recipes or products. Bill actually reads the ingredients in a recipe and seems pretty confident when he comments, "This sounds really good." Right! That comment subsequently led us to our discovery of Phyllo dough and the education of what, where, when, and the how of Phyllo! Or not!

Our first bit of education came in just finding the dough in the grocery store. Finally we asked for help and a clerk directed us to the freezer section. Our grocery store actually had the product and we brought that interesting looking box home and as instructed "Keep frozen." I researched the internet for recipes. Almost immediately I found *Apple Strudel*. Ah ha! Sounded really good and has pure German appeal. I printed that sucker out. I studied the recipe and that's when I began to read about the difficulty of working with Phyllo dough. But, like usual, warn me that something might be difficult and I must surely have the experience. We scanned the procedure. As instructed, we took the box containing the frozen phyllo from the freezer and placed it in the refrigerator overnight for use the next day.

THE COUNTDOWN BEGINS

While Bill peels the apples, I gather the necessary ingredients: sugar, cinnamon, nutmeg, butter, bread crumbs, pecans, lemon, lemon juice, apple juice. We chat our way through the above activities. Bill has now peeled the Galas and has chopped the apples into one-fourth inch pieces. As directed, we toss them into the mixture of sugar, cinnamon, nutmeg, salt, lemon zest, lemon juice, apple juice and set the mixture aside. Meanwhile, I have toasted the bread crumbs in a small skillet along with a bit of butter and added the cracked pecans, cinnamon, and sugar. Also set aside as instructed. According to the instructions, we melted more butter and have it "at ready" along with a pastry brush. We are big on instructions.

NOW WE GO FOR THE PHYLLO

All this time the excitement has been building. I opened the box and took out one plastic wrapped roll of dough and instead of first re-reading the instructions on how to handle these almost transparent and fragile sheets of dough, I jumped right in and—okay—this is what happened:

I enjoy working while seated at our medium sized butcher block located in the middle of our tiny kitchen. When Bill asks, "What can I do?" I tell him to thoroughly wet down a dish towel because "we need to keep these sheets damp." (I knew I read that somewhere.) So, Bill wet down and squeezed the extra water out of a clean towel and he asks, "Now what?" Meanwhile, I have placed in front of me on the butcher block a long sheet of parchment paper to work on. I had also placed a sheet of parchment paper onto the jelly roll pan we'll use it to bake our strudel. The oven is warming to 350 degrees.

Bill is still standing there, waiting with the damp towel, "What should I do with this?" he asks again.

"Frankly I don't know, I just remember the instructions said it was important." I honestly can't remember for sure where or what, so I say, "Just spread it in the jelly roll pan on top of the parchment paper." Meanwhile, I have opened up the 12-inch scroll of Phyllo and unrolled them directly onto the butcher block and covered it immediately with plastic wrap.

PUTTING IT ALL TOGETHER

I take my first sheet of paper thin, almost see-though Phyllo. The first sheet came off the stack seemingly okay but it also came apart in my hands and most of it stayed stuck onto the pile of sheets. In frustration, I drop the torn mess onto the towel in the jelly roll pan and try to lift off another sheet and, since I am not too gentle, it comes apart in my hands again. I repeat this action again. I destroyed three more sheets of dough and they are in miserable heaps on the damp towel/jelly roll pan. Not to be defeated, I try to straighten them out in vain but I nevertheless haphazardly apply a little bit of melted butter to the miserable heap of dough. Finally, I manage to gently and successfully lift off an unbroken sheet and I gently place it on top of the three miserable heaps of dough and I brush melted butter on the sheet—brushing away from me until the entire sheet is buttered. Next, we sprinkled some of the bread crumb mixture over the buttered sheet.

(I am feeling hopeful now. I've got the hang of it, I think.)

"Okay, Bill, let me get another sheet." He lifts the plastic wrap to assist me in that and . . . Oh no! Another sheet is stuck! Same song, second verse: we destroy another three sheets as before. *Idiot, be gentle!* I mentally remind myself.

Finally, I am out of melted butter. I am out of the bread crumb mixture. There is a lot of dough left over.

"What now?" asks Bill. "What's next?"

I shrug, "Hell, I don't know! I'll just try to redeem these apples."

Saying that, I take the waiting bowl with the apple mixture and just dump the whole thing onto the truly messy looking sheets just lying there, embarrassing me. When I try to roll the whole thing up jelly roll style—(I vaguely remembered this next step in making strudel)—by lifting the wet towel everything seems to go wrong. The entire conglomeration just seems to get out of control. The apple mixture had drawn a lot of liquid and it began to run off the pile of dough and onto the wet towel. But, not to be defeated, we finally managed to "round up" all the stray pieces of apple and juice now strewn all over the jelly roll pan. I try to lift up the mass. I ask Bill to just pull away the wet towel from under this mess—soaking up the run off juices. Somehow how, magically, I managed to lift up the now misshapen loaf containing that pile of apples and dough and it now rests on the sheet of parchment paper. I take one look at the sad jumble and I hear voices in my head saying *Idiot. Idiot. When will you learn to read all the instructions?*

Still, I will not give up. I melt more butter and then we take sheet after sheet of Phyllo and butter each one and lay it over the mess to cover it all up as best as we can. We then began to tuck the Phyllo dough all around and under—forming a foot long loaf of diced apple stuff. Finally, with a little more tucking here and there, I brushed the entire thing once more with melted butter and along with my apologies, I sprinkle it all with more sugar and cinnamon. We slapped that sucker into the oven and I predicted to Bill that I am sure the entire jelly roll pan will soon be filled with all that apple juice. I feel pretty much licked by Phyllo dough!

Bill just gives me that, "Maybe we should have read the instructions again." I raised my eyebrows, shake my head, and I go back and re-read the directions. I discover that the wet towel should have been placed on top of the pile of waiting Phyllo dough and then the sheet of plastic over the wet towel.

THE END RESULT

After the instructed 35 minutes of baking time, we get up enough courage to peek at our baking creation. There is no apple juice in sight! Wonder of wonders! Only then do I remember reading that the reason for the bread crumbs is to soak up the juice! Hmmm. Maybe. I'm thinking, maybe we have rescued . . . I add another few minutes to the baking because, I reason, that is one big pile of cubed apples we have inside that log.

THE OUTCOME

Number one, the wonderful sweet scents of cinnamon and melted butter baking in the oven served to sooth our wounded pride. Bill seems to take it all in stride as we clean up the mess. . . some of it on the floor around the butcher block. It is time to re- move the final product from the oven. It looks wonderful, smells great. We place our creation on the waiting cooling rack. We both shrug and agree that we can hardly wait to taste this *giant strudel*.

I sliced diagonally through the apple stuffed loaf with a sharp bread knife. My first cut—about four inches from the end of the log—as instructed—I cut in a gentle sawing motion as the baked top sheets of Phyllo crumble and fall onto the parchment paper. I cut off two one inch thick slices and lifted them onto a plate Bill is hold- ing over the pan. "That looks really good, Sweetie!" He is smiling.

"I'm astounded!" I reply. "Maybe we've pulled off a successful major goof-up cover-up. This truly looks scrumptious!"

And it was! In spite of all the mistakes, we created a wonderful delectable dessert. We have already bought another box of Phyllo and more apples and we will try this again. Only next time we will place the wet towel where it belongs—on top of the piled sheets of dough. We will probably still make a mess but at least next time we'll know what to expect. We are also thinking of other possible strudels like—peach—maybe cherry—maybe—I know—I'll go to the Internet for more recipes and—

That's the story of
BILL AND MAE GO STRUDEL

My Final Recipe

Party Time Punch

Recipe from Dolly Rose

Get the celebration started right!

2 medium cans pineapple juice   1 fifth dark rum
1 box frozen strawberries   1 fifth light rum
2 cans frozen orange juice   1 ½ pints peach brandy
1 #2 can chunk pineapple   1 fifth champagne

Combine all ingredients and dilute with water if necessary. If desired, add red food coloring.

Traditional German Christmas family reunions always seem to center around a table. On the back row is the author's brother, Otto (now deceased) and his wife Lillian, and Bill Nelson. In the front row is "baby brother" Warren Hahn and his wife Katie, and deceased brother Oliver's widow Helen Hahn. Recipes have been exchanged between the family for more than sixty years.

Index

BARS AND CANDY

CAKES AND FROSTINGS

CLASSIC COLLECTORS' RECIPES

COOKIES

FAVORITE SPECIALTY DESSERTS

MAIN COURSES AND CASSEROLES

PIES

SIDE DISHES

SOUPS AND CHOWDERS

BONUSES

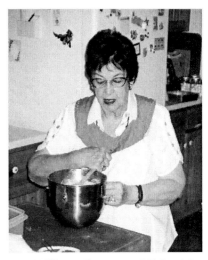

ALORA (MAE) DURDEN-NELSON retired in 1997 after twenty-seven years as the Comfort School District's elementary children's librarian where she authored and produced puppet, marionette, and/or stage plays twice a year, every year, with fifth and sixth grade students for her Elementary Library Children's Theater project. One play, "The Case of the Easter Villians," was published in *Plays Inc.* magazine.

She has served on several community service boards, including Comfort Chamber of Commerce (seven years); Comfort Public Education Foundation board, writing public relations news articles, and served on the scholarship committee; she served on the board of the Comfort Public Library, was elected president in 1995, and served until her retirement from public school. Most recently, she was secretary of the board of the Comfort Area Youth Commission where she also served as a grant writer and editor of the CAYC newsletter. The Rising Star Masonic Lodge of Center Point, Texas, honored her with a Community Builder Award in 1998. Also, the Comfort Heritage Foundation recognized her with the 2007 award for "recording history" in the book, *When Saints Go Marching*, the 100-year history of St. Boniface Episcopal Church in Comfort. Durden-Nelson has been a member of the Southwest Chapter of Book Writers and Illustrators since 1986 and is a member of the Texas Author's Speakers Bureau.

Her earlier writing credits include being a stringer/freelance reporter and Society Editor for the *Kerrville Daily Times*. In 1968 she compiled and wrote the history of the Immanuel Lutheran Church in Comfort, *With Eternal Glory*, and authored two newspaper series for the *Comfort News* on the "History of the Comfort PTA" and "Why Voter Registration?"

182

Durden-Nelson's first retirement-writing venture, requested by the YMCA in 1999, was to research the history of the 1,100 acre Robert's Ranch near Comfort and then produce a brochure for the ranch to encourage Boy and Girl Scout troops primitive camping, field trips for educational, historical, archeological, rock-climbing and birding adventures.

Durden-Nelson's first book, *I Just Called Her Momma* (Eakin Press, 2000), was published in 2003 and she has written and published a book a year ever since: *Son of Defiance*; the sequel *Genesis—Beginning Again*; *When Saints Go Marching* (a commissioned work); *Four Boys, Two Canoes, and the Guadalupe River*; and *There's a Raccoon in My Bathroom*, released in 2010. Her last book, *The Little House with a Big Story*, was released in November 2010. All her books have been published by Eakin Press, Waco, Texas. *At Home at the Range* is her latest book.

Durden-Nelson and her husband Bill Nelson have given book talks throughout Texas since 2003. Contact may be made through her website: www.MaeDurdenNelson.com

WILLIAM (BILL) WATKINS NELSON was born December 1, 1926, in Oklahoma and grew up in Aransas Pass, Texas. He served in the U.S. Navy during World War II and the Korean conflict. He graduated from Texas Tech School of Architecture May 21, 1951. He was employed by Dexter Hamon, Architect in Corpus Christi. He married Kit Nelson in 1950.

In 1960 Bill became the first resident manager of Camp Capers, an Episcopal Church Camp located between Comfort and Waring, Texas. He spent ten years in service there. He then became the Resident Architect and Department Head of Drafting at Southwestern Engineering Company in Comfort in 1970 and retired after twenty years. He was then employed as the business manager of Camp Stewart in Hunt, Texas, until his final retirement in 1991. He lost his wife to cancer in 1996.

Bill served on several boards in Comfort, Texas. He was president of the board, Comfort Public Library; Kendall County Historical Foundation; Comfort Historical Foundation; a member of the book committee publishing a history of the Comfort schools; served on the Bishop's Committee of the St. Boniface Episcopal Church in Comfort for many years; and served on the Comfort Independent School District's school board. Bill served on the Kendall County Water Control and Improvement District for twenty-eight years. Bill also designed the memorial bell tower located in front of the Comfort Middle School, as well as several business and residential buildings in Comfort.

He was awarded the Comfort Chamber of Commerce Outstanding Citizen Award in 1995. He was the "piano man" with the Comfort Little Theater for years and is remembered for his Queen Bee and Julia Child skits.

Bill Nelson and Mae Durden were married in 1997. He has done the photography for Mae's books and is the business manager of their Winsome Merging Marketing Company since 2003. They have traveled more than 40,000 miles throughout the U.S., and have traveled together with book talks and book signings. The couple has also recorded three CDs, two in Nashville and one "in house" with Rough Diamond Productions featuring Bill at the piano and accompanying Mae singing old show tunes. They recently retired from Joyful Noise, a small musical group with Bill at the piano, accompanying a banjo, guitars, mandolin, harmonica and singers. Bill and Mae entertain regularly at nursing homes in Comfort, Kerrville, and Fredericksburg.